Mahle

HIS LIFE & MUS

Stephen Johnson

Mahler

HIS LIFE & MUSIC

Stephen Johnson

sourcebooks
mediaFusion

An Imprint of Sourcebooks Inc.®
Naperville, Illinois

Published by Sourcebooks MediaFusion, an imprint of Sourcebooks, Inc.
P.O. Box 4410, Naperville, Illinois 60567-4410
(630) 961-3900
Fax: (630) 961-2168
www.sourcebooks.com

Originally published in the UK by Naxos Books.

Printed and bound in the United States of America.
BVG   10 9 8 7 6 5 4 3 2 1

Author's Acknowledgments

The books listed in the Bibliography have all been helpful, and readers will find that each one has plenty to add to the comments and observations made in the main text. I would also like to thank those who have personally enriched my understanding of Mahler, whether in professional interviews or in private conversation. They include the conductors Sir Simon Rattle, Klaus Tennstedt, Günter Wand, Gilbert Kaplan, Riccardo Chailly and Benjamin Zander; the composers Robert Simpson, Colin Matthews, Anthony Payne, James MacMillan and Gerard McBurney; the writers and musicologists Michael Kennedy, Paul Banks, Edward Seckerson, Robert Maycock and Harriet Smith; and producers Andrew Keener and Gautam Rangarajan. Not least I should like to thank my wife Kate, whose sharply focused criticism and more qualified enthusiasm for Mahler have more than once forced me to rethink my own position: always essential when dealing with a subject as complex and elusive as music.

Visit the dedicated website for *Mahler: His Life & Music* and gain free access to the following:
- Hours of extra music to listen to
- Music by many of Mahler's contemporaries
- A timeline of Mahler's life, set alongside contemporary events in arts, culture and history

To access this you will need:
- ISBN: 1843791145
- Password: Lieder

About the Life & Music Series

The Life & Music series presents fully rounded, accessible portraits of composers through an ideal mix of media: words, pictures, and the music itself. With its extensive catalogue of classical recordings, its experience of the classical music world, its expertise in the use of the Internet, and its growing reputation for educational material, Naxos is ideally placed to provide richly illustrated and authoritative biographies of the great musical figures in the western tradition.

About Sourcebooks MediaFusion

Launched with the 1998 New York Times bestseller *We Interrupt This Broadcast* and formally founded in 2000, Sourcebooks MediaFusion is the nation's leading publisher of mixed-media books. This revolutionary imprint is dedicated to creating original content—be it audio, video, CD-ROM, or Web—that is fully integrated with the books we create. The result, we hope, is a new, richer, eye-opening, thrilling experience with books for our readers. Our experiential books have become both bestsellers and classics in their subjects, including poetry (*Poetry Speaks*), children's books (*Poetry Speaks to Children*), history (*We Shall Overcome*), sports (*And The Crowd Goes Wild*), the plays of William Shakespeare, and more. See what's new from us at www.sourcebooks.com.

Contents

Preface

There are those who say that music is, or ought to be, self-explanatory – or that even if it isn't, there comes a point where, in the words of Duke Ellington, 'too much talk stinks the place out.' Analysis of, say, a fugue by J.S. Bach can deepen one's understanding of its intellectual processes. Knowledge of Bach's cultural background and religious beliefs can throw light on specific details, or even on why he chose the fugal form in the first place. Yet, one can love and be moved by the sound it makes, and even appreciate its basic formal elegance, without knowing anything about the mind that created it, or the musical techniques employed.

With Mahler it is different. It is true that much of his music can be enjoyed 'innocently', that the listener can simply revel in its sensuous beauty and imaginative brilliance. The exquisite floating strings and harp textures that open the famous **Adagietto** in the Fifth Symphony are simply captivating as sound – no explanation needed. But almost invariably in a Mahler work the listener will sooner or later be forced to ask: why does he do *that*? Why is a passage of rapt contemplation suddenly interrupted by a violent emotional outburst, or a trivial little tune, or something that sounds alarmingly like mockery? Why does Mahler seem to set out purposefully on a journey, only to change direction suddenly? At such moments, it is hard to resist the impression that there

CD 2
track 2
www.naxosbooks.com

is something in particular that Mahler wants to tell us: that he has a message, something urgently personal or perhaps even philosophical, that he wants us to contemplate.

Mahler's letters and recorded comments make it clear that he did, even if he found it difficult to put this message into words. When his first two symphonies appeared, he provided them with elaborate literary programmes to guide the listener towards what he felt their meaning was. The trouble here was that he could be taken rather literally; one woman even pressed him to tell her what the afterlife was like (he must know, she insisted, since he had portrayed it so movingly in his 'Resurrection' Symphony). There were times when Mahler must have felt inclined to agree with the composer Felix Mendelssohn, who wrote that 'the thoughts which are expressed to me by music that I love are not too indefinite to be put into words, but on the contrary, too definite'. In other words, musical thoughts are real enough, but they are *musical* thoughts. They express things and obey laws that are peculiar to music.

So how can a book like this help the listener, especially one who may respond deeply to music but who has little or no knowledge of specialist musical theory or practice? As I hope to show, there are few composers besides Mahler whose music is so deeply involved with the events and experiences of their personal lives. Knowing who Mahler was – where he came from, what his unique joys and sufferings were, what his 'take' was on the world in which he found himself – can help us to understand the 'why' of his music. Yet, in the end, there is much more to Mahler's great symphonies and songs than autobiography or philosophy in sound: much more. Understanding the connection between 'the man that suffers and the mind that creates', as T.S. Eliot put it, can take us a long way in the right direction, but it is by no means the end of the story. Getting to know a piece of music can be an adventure, one that may take us to surprising places or bring unexpected revelations. This book can provide signposts along the first stages of the road; after that, it is entirely up to the listener to discover where, imaginatively speaking, that road leads. There is no final, absolute truth. We may all hear the same notes, but each of us will experience something different in them. It is Mahler who speaks to us; the feelings and thoughts he stimulates in us will be different from those aroused by any other kind of music. It is also true that, in the words of the philosopher Ernst Bloch, 'when we listen to music, what we hear is ourselves'. Thus the final message of this book should be: 'over to you'. As you listen to the music featured on the two CDs accompanying this book, you can decide for yourself whether the writer's verbal signposts have been helpful, or whether the music takes you on a different kind of mental journey. In the end, the message of Mahler's music is what you find in it for yourself. No one can tell you that you are right or wrong.

There is, however, one point on which I would like to reassure the non-specialist reader: this is emphatically not a book for musicians or musicologists. Technical terminology is kept to a bare minimum. The great 'anti-musicologist' Hans Keller used to say: 'You should never use a musical term until you absolutely can't do without it'. Having to explain a musical concept in language that an intelligent layman may grasp can be exciting, refreshing, even humbling. Often it turns out that the use of jargon conceals inadequate understanding of the subject matter. Ultimately, though, understanding Mahler and his music has nothing whatsoever to do with labelling his works' contents correctly, according to this or that school of musical thought. It is a matter for the human heart; and, as far as that goes, we are all experts.

Chapter 1
Three Times Homeless

Three Times Homeless

I am three times homeless: a native of Bohemia in Austria;
an Austrian among Germans; a Jew throughout the world.

Of all the remarks attributed to Gustav Mahler, this one is perhaps the most famous. From a geographical and ethnic perspective it is, of course, completely accurate. Throughout his life, Mahler was conscious of being an outsider, never quite 'at home'. However, the saying also contains an important spiritual truth. Here Mahler clearly identifies himself with the archetypal romantic figure of 'The Wanderer', celebrated in the titles of three songs by his beloved Schubert, as well as in the same composer's famous 'Wanderer' Fantasy for Piano and great song cycle *Winterreise* ('Winter Journey'). Mahler may also have had a much older figure at the back of his mind: the legendary 'Wandering Jew', according to tradition punished for mocking Christ as he carried his cross by being condemned to wander over the face of the earth until Judgement Day. In the overwhelmingly Roman Catholic Austrian Empire, anti-Semitism was, as we would now say, 'institutionalised'. The Church still taught that the Jewish people were collectively responsible for the death of Christ, and that their dispersal throughout the world (the so-called 'diaspora') was their divinely ordained punishment. Wherever he went, and no matter how much success he achieved as an artist, Mahler continued to run up against anti-Jewish attitudes – expressed sometimes in the form of mild, unthinking prejudice (routine 'Jewish jokes') and at other times as pure, virulent hostility.

Embracing the World

One of the most common accusations made against Mahler as a composer is that he was a 'self-dramatiser', that his music is unashamedly self-centered, so bound up with his own agonies and ecstasies that he misses the quality of 'universality' held by some to distinguish the very greatest works of art. Perhaps this is so, but one could also argue that there are many roads to the universal, and that in the hands of a genius of Mahler's stature, self-dramatisation may be one of them. Another famous remark attributed to Mahler was recorded by the Finnish composer Jean Sibelius (1865–1957) after the two men met in Helsinki in 1907 and, in Sibelius's words, 'discussed all the great questions of music thoroughly'. Sibelius argued for what may be called the 'classical' view on the subject of the symphony: 'I said that I admired its severity of style and the profound logic that created an inner connection between all the motifs.' Mahler's response was characteristically explosive: 'No, the symphony must be like the world. It must embrace everything.' Embracing everything meant reflecting *all* that was in the world – good and evil, high and low, exalted and banal – and reflecting it through the prism of his own personality. It is that unmistakably personal stamp that makes Mahler so endlessly fascinating for large numbers of music lovers. As the American composer Aaron Copland put it:

When all is said, there remains something extraordinarily touching about the man's work, something that makes one

3

willing to put up with the weaknesses. Perhaps this is because his music is so very Mahler-like in every detail. All his nine symphonies are suffused with personality – he had his own way of saying and doing everything. The irascible scherzos, the heaven-storming calls in the brass, the special quality of his communings with nature, the gentle melancholy of a traditional passage, the gargantuan Ländler, the pages of an incredible loneliness – all these, combined with his histrionics, an inner warmth, and the will to evoke the largest forms and the grandest musical thoughts, add up to one of the most fascinating composer-personalities of modern times.

One might ask why Mahler isn't described as 'self-absorbed' rather than 'fascinating'. This is partly because the music can be so searingly beautiful, so vividly dramatic and so brilliantly inventive, but also because, at the same time as we recognize Mahler in everything he does, we may also recognize ourselves. Just as Mahler is uniquely himself, he is also Everyman: the music does 'embrace everything', and the personal becomes the universal.

All this affects the way in which Mahler's music is discussed and evaluated. Although it is possible to analyse any of Mahler's symphonies in the same way that one might approach a symphony by Brahms (identifying the leading themes, showing how they are developed against an evolving harmonic background, and so on), the listener to Mahler will soon encounter details or events that refuse to fit in with such an abstract analytical scheme. The music cries out for some kind of larger interpretation: what is Mahler trying to *say*? It is on that question that this book will concentrate. Time after time it seems that an explanation can only be found by referring to Mahler's own remarks and to the events of his

The music cries out for some kind of larger interpretation: what is Mahler trying to *say*?

life. In other words, in order to understand that process of self-dramatization, it is necessary to understand what made Mahler the unique 'self' that he was.

Mahler's World: Origins and Background

Fortunately, Mahler revealed a fair amount about his childhood to those who were closest to him, much of which has survived in the form of written reminiscences. The basic facts are easily accessible. Mahler was born on 7 July 1860, in the Bohemian town of Kalischt (now Kaliště, in the Czech Republic). In those days the Czech lands were all governed from the Austrian Imperial capital, Vienna, with German the official language. Speaking Czech was not encouraged, but emergent nationalism had given the language a subversive vitality, so that nationalistically inclined middle-class Czechs such as the composer Bedřich Smetana (1824–1884) felt obliged to learn it. The communities in which Mahler grew up may have been largely German-speaking, but his being 'a native of Bohemia in Austria' would have made him feel provincial, almost a foreigner.

That Mahler should later have felt out of place as 'an Austrian among Germans' indicated how much the political world was changing around the time of his birth. Until the mid-nineteenth century, the distinction between what we now call Austria and Germany was far from clear. For centuries Vienna had been the capital of a vast, sprawling and rather loose confederation of states known as the 'Holy Roman Empire', a huge territory that had included at different times not only German-speaking territories but also Czechoslovakia, Poland, Hungary, large parts of the Balkans, Northern Italy and even Spain. Following the final defeat of Napoleon in 1815, Austria had played the dominant role in the 'German

Confederation', under the leadership of the Austrian diplomat Prince Clemens von Metternich (1773–1859). But the rising power and influence of Prussia forced Austria to withdraw from German affairs in 1866, when Prussia defeated Austria in the so-called 'Seven Weeks War'. Austria responded in 1867 by creating the 'dual monarchy': a strange political compromise designed to pacify Hungarian nationalism of Austria-Hungary, while maintaining Vienna as the center of power. This made the Habsburg Franz Joseph I both Emperor of Austria and King of Hungary, a title reflected in the official royal seal 'K & K' (*Kaiserlich und Königlich* – 'Imperial and Royal'). As such, Franz Joseph stamped his authority on most of the Czech-speaking lands, Italy, Poland, Romania, Russia and large parts of what is now called 'the former Yugoslavia'.

In the first half of the nineteenth century, the right of abode for Jews in Austria-Hungary was strictly regulated. After 1848, the great 'Year of Revolutions', Jews tended to be regarded with particular suspicion by conservatives, as a potential 'enemy within', not naturally sharing the national interests of their compatriots; in 1860, the year of Mahler's birth, however, the laws were somewhat relaxed. By the standards of his time Franz Joseph was not especially anti-Semitic, and he seems to have regarded the 'assimilation' of Jews at all levels of Austrian society as moderately acceptable. This was excellent news for Gustav's father Bernhard Mahler (1827–1889). An intelligent, ambitious man, he started his professional life as a coachman but he was conspicuously keen to 'improve' himself, particularly by reading. He soon acquired the nickname of 'the coachbox scholar' among his peers. In 1857 Bernhard obtained the lease on a small inn in Kalischt. That same year he married Marie Hermann, ten years younger and the second daughter of a local soap-

The idea that Mahler grew up in poverty turns out to have been a myth, although one which may have romantically enhanced his reputation as the 'poor Jewish boy made good'.

boiler, Abraham Hermann. As soon as the laws governing right of abode for Jews were relaxed, Bernhard moved to the Bohemian but predominantly German-speaking town of Iglau (now Jihlava), taking with him Marie and the four-month-old Gustav. In Iglau – bigger than Kalischt and with a significant industrial base – Bernhard acquired a spirit factory and prospered, soon becoming a pillar of the middle-class Jewish community and attending the synagogue regularly with his family. The idea that Mahler grew up in poverty turns out to have been a myth, although

Gustav's father
Bernhard Mahler

one which may have romantically enhanced his reputation as the 'poor Jewish boy made good'. Gustav was effectively Bernhard's 'first-born' – a previous child having died in early infancy – and at times Bernhard took a special fatherly pride in him. Although he may not have seen Gustav's soon-evident musicality as the basis of a career, he certainly considered it a potential social asset.

Home-life: Tragedy and Dreams

The Mahler home was by no means unfavorable to the growth of young Gustav's musical talent, yet there must have been times when it was a difficult place in which to grow up for any child, gifted or not. Gustav was the second of fourteen children born to Bernhard and Marie Mahler, which means that his mother must have been either pregnant or recovering from childbirth for most of his youth, making it difficult for little Gustav to attract her attention for very long. There was death in the house too. When Gustav was fourteen, his younger brother Ernst died after a long fatal illness (diagnosed as hydrocardia), during which Gustav nursed him, sitting by his bedside, reading him stories, for week after week. This experience has often been cited to explain the mature Mahler's obsession with death in his music – particularly with the deaths of children, which form the subject of his great song cycle *Kindertotenlieder* (*Songs on the Deaths of Children*). It is worth remembering that infant mortality was much more common in nineteenth-century Europe than it is today, especially in the poorer outposts of the Austro-Hungarian Empire. The composer Anton Bruckner (1824–1896), who was to be something of a mentor during Mahler's years at the Vienna Conservatory, was the first of twelve children, of whom only five survived infancy. Like Mahler, Bruckner was, in T.S. Eliot's famous line, 'much possessed by death'. Modern readers may not relate to the sentimental depiction of Little Nell's death in Charles Dickens's *Old Curiosity Shop* (1840– 1), but Dickens was likewise the product of an age that had to confront the specter of childhood mortality.

That Marie Mahler bore her husband fourteen children suggests that their relationship was especially loving, but Gustav Mahler's reports of it indicate otherwise. Some of the composer's recollections were recorded by his wife, Alma, in her account of their own relationship, *Memories and Letters*:

> *[Mahler] dreamed his way through family life and childhood. He saw nothing of the unending tortures his mother had to endure from the brutality of his father, who ran after every servant, domineered over his delicate wife and flogged the children.*

If Mahler 'saw nothing' on account of his day-dreaming, it is surprising that he was able to recall so vividly his mother's 'unending tortures'. Possibly, Alma was here relying on the testimony of Mahler's sister Justine ('Justi'), to whom he remained close throughout his adult life. But the memories do seem to have been Mahler's own, at least in part. In 1910 Mahler famously consulted the father of psychoanalysis Sigmund Freud, who remembered, in a letter written fifteen years later, some of what Mahler had told him:

His father, apparently a brutal person, treated his wife very badly, and when Mahler was a young boy there was an especially painful scene between them. It became quite unbearable to the boy, who rushed away from the house. At that moment, however, a hurdy-gurdy in the street was grinding out the popular Viennese air O, du lieber Augustin. In Mahler's opinion the conjunction of high tragedy and light amusement was from then on inextricably fixed in his mind, and the one mood inevitably brought the other with it.

Mahler and his sister Justine in Vienna, 1899

Events like the one described above can be illuminating when Mahler's music confronts us with that question: what is he trying to *say*? Given that Mahler dwells so much on themes of childhood (the 'child's view of heaven' song that forms the last movement of his Fourth Symphony, or the song cycle

9

Kindertotenlieder), he was surely right when he claimed that these early experiences left an indelible mark on his music.

One might add that it left an 'indelible mark' on him too, but to what degree? Were the experiences all as negative as the accounts given by Alma Mahler and Freud suggest? As a conductor Mahler could be, frankly, a bully: 'brutal' was a word used about him more than once. Professionally, he could also be ambitious, cunning and duplicitous in pursuit of his aims and ideals. It is easy to recognize Bernhard's behavior in Mahler's dealings with the staff, casts and managers of the various opera houses for which he worked. His mother, on the other hand, left a different kind of imprint.

Mahler remembered her as loving (when pregnancy and parenthood allowed), delicate and a victim – and he idolized her memory. Perhaps even her perpetual limp was responsible for the strange gait that Alma and several others observed in the adult Mahler: a change of pace every three or four steps, somewhere between walking and skipping. It is not difficult to find passages in Mahler's music that seem to evoke the sacred memory of Marie Mahler: the ecstatic, yearning hymns to the Virgin Mary (Maria/Marie: surely significant) in Part Two of the choral Eighth Symphony, or the grief-laden mother, struggling to come to terms with the loss of her children, in *Kindertotenlieder*.

> As a conductor Mahler could be, frankly, a bully: 'brutal' was a word used about him more than once.

As a boy, Mahler's dreaminess was pronounced. Alma records how Bernhard Mahler was once taking little Gustav for a walk in the woods when suddenly, remembering some unfinished business, he told his son to wait for him while he hurried home. According to the story, Bernhard became so absorbed in what he was doing that he forgot his son until much later. Then, horrified at his own negligence, he rushed back to rescue him. Returning to the place where he had left

Gustav Mahler in 1865, aged 5

him, Bernhard found Gustav still in the same spot, apparently lost in thought. This might explain what Copland called 'the special quality of [Mahler's] communings with nature' in his music, and that absorption in nature lasted his whole lifetime. He was at his happiest writing music surrounded by the sights and sounds of the Austrian Alps (provided they were not too obtrusive).

The adult Mahler also tended to go off in a dream, not just when alone but even in good company. This is the musician who remained buried in one of his own scores for hours on a motionless train, oblivious to the fact that he was not moving; or the man who often seemed to absent himself in the middle of conversations – some thought enchantingly, others rudely. Here, too, we recognise the composer of the song 'Ich bin der Welt abhanden gekommen' ('I am lost to the world') from the five *Rückert Lieder*.

> **He was at his happiest writing music surrounded by the sights and sounds of the Austrian Alps.**

The sounds of nature abound in Mahler's music: from the evocations of birdcalls near the opening of the First Symphony, to the rippling harps and clarinets suggesting the singing to the brook in the final song of *Das Lied von der Erde*, to the use of cowbells in the Sixth and Seventh symphonies. Another potent childhood influence was the sound of military fanfares and band music, stemming from the nearby town barracks at Iglau. Years later Mahler told his close confidante Natalie Bauer-Lechner about one of his earliest memories of the soldiers and their music:

One day when I was not yet four a funny thing happened. A military band, something I delighted in all my childhood, came marching past our house one morning. I no sooner heard it than I shot out of the living room. Wearing scarcely more than a chemise (they hadn't dressed me yet) I trailed

after the soldiers with my little accordion until some time later a couple of the ladies from nearby discovered me at the market-place. By that time I was feeling a bit frightened and they said they would only promise to take me home if I played them something the soldiers had been playing, on my accordion. I did so straight away, upon a fruit stall where they set me, to the utter delight of the market women, cooks and other bystanders. At that, amid shouts and laughter they bore me back to my parents, who were already in a great panic over my disappearance.

Mahler's home at Iglau

As with the story about little Mahler in the woods, absorbed in nature, the reader may well feel that if it isn't true, then it ought to be. So much in that little vignette is characteristically 'Mahlerian'. There is the boy's simple joy in music that causes him to forget himself, then the fear and separation anxiety, then salvation from two sources: music, and the women who take him home to safety. The story also helps to account for the fanfares and lively march tunes that crop up in Mahler's music over and over again. Distant fanfares are the first 'primal' sounds to be heard in the slow, mysterious introduction to the First Symphony's opening movement, alongside the woodwind birdcalls. Then there are the exultant martial flourishes and side-drum tattoos in the first movement of the Third Symphony, originally entitled 'Summer marches in'.

'A Born Musician'

As well as relating stories of how the music of man and nature impressed him, Mahler indicated that his father could sometimes be a beneficial influence. When Mahler was about five or six, Bernhard found him tinkering on an old piano. He was sufficiently impressed and sent his son for lessons. Within three years Mahler had advanced so far that he was able to give piano lessons himself, and at the age of ten he gave his first public recital in Iglau. Concerned for Gustav's wider education, Bernhard sent him to study at the Gymnasium (Grammar School) in Prague, arranging for him to stay with a musical family, the Grünfelds; Mahler, however, was bullied at school and neglected at the Grünfeld home. He later told Alma that he had 'accepted it all as a matter of course', but when Bernhard heard about his son's ill-treatment he set off for Prague immediately and took Gustav back to Iglau.

At home Mahler continued to make striking progress on the piano. In the spring of 1875 a local estate manager heard him play Beethoven's Piano Sonata 'Les Adieux' ('The Farewells') – already something of a party-piece – and recommended that Mahler be taken to the Vienna Conservatory. Reluctantly, Bernhard complied. The fifteen-year-old Mahler was granted an audition with the Professor of Piano, Julius Epstein (1832– 1926). Thirty-six years later, in the year of Mahler's death,

Mahler in 1872 with a cousin (standing)

Epstein recalled that first meeting:

I was giving lectures at the Conservatory when a visitor was announced. A man came to me, and asked for my advice. He was accompanied by a boy of about fourteen or fifteen. 'My name is Mahler, and I have spirit factory in Iglau,' began the elderly man. He gestured towards the boy. 'This is my son Gustav. He is absolutely set on being a musician. I would prefer him to study at school at the technical college and the university so that eventually he can take over my factory, but the boy does not want to.' ...I cannot even remember what he played, and at most it lasted five minutes. But my judgement was firm. I put it in these words: 'Herr Mahler, your son is a born musician!' He looked at me surprised, and even somewhat dismayed, and said: 'Forgive me, Herr Professor, but just now you said it was difficult to decide on a person's future. You have barely listened for five minutes, and you have already made up your mind.' 'I am not being unreasonable,' I explained. 'In this case I could not be wrong. This young man has spirit, but he will never take over his father's spirit factory.'

Conservatory Years: Bruckner's Disciples

Mahler entered the Vienna Conservatory in September 1875. Epstein was his teacher for piano, and it is an indication of his respect for his young pupil that he later engaged him to teach his own son, Richard. Other teachers included Robert Fuchs for harmony and Franz Krenn for composition. Composition teaching was a much more formal matter in the nineteenth century than it is today. Was Mahler a good pupil? The accurate answer is probably 'yes and no'. Robert Fuchs told Alma Mahler that Gustav 'always played truant and yet there was nothing he couldn't do. It is said that his fellow students were soon calling him 'another Schubert', which suggests that he was already composing songs. Unfortunately, a great deal of the music that Mahler wrote during this period has been lost. Perhaps to placate his father, he continued his general education at the Iglau Gymnasium, which he seems to have funded by giving more piano lessons.

Apart from those putative songs, Mahler composed a fair quantity of chamber music, a very practical choice of medium in a conservatory with so many talented young performers to hand. The first movement of a piano quartet in A minor survives from this period. It is skilfully written, and its turbulent, highly expressive minor-key character suggests that Mahler was quite clear about the kind of music he wanted to write. The work may be rather stylized (its easily identifiable gestures of Austro-German Romanticism have led some critics to call it 'pastiche'), and yet the mature Mahler, too, would often evoke the stylistic conventions of other composers and other ages. The first movement of his Fourth Symphony, for example, could be described as one of the first great exercises in neo-Classicism.

> The first movement of a piano quartet in A minor survives from this period. It is skilfully written, and its turbulent, highly expressive minor-key character suggests that Mahler was quite clear about the kind of music he wanted to write.

Mahler also made significant friendships with some of his fellow students, like the future great Lieder composer Hugo Wolf (1860–1903). Mahler and Wolf remained close until they fell out over the text of an opera, *Rübezahl*, which they both independently considered setting to music. There was also the brilliant but deeply unstable Hans Rott (1858–1884), who died insane at the age of twenty-six. Rott's remarkable Symphony in E (1878–80) almost certainly influenced Mahler: there are striking echoes of it in Mahler's own First Symphony. Another important friendship was with Rudolf Krzyzanowski (1859–1911), who, like Mahler, would become a conductor, working for a while as Mahler's assistant at the Hamburg Opera in the mid-1890s. All of them as students were very short of money and frequently pooled their resources. The food parcels and gifts of clothing from Mahler's parents were particularly prized. After 1876 Julius Epstein generously helped Mahler with his tuition fees, and sent as many piano pupils as he could in Mahler's direction.

The young men were all united in their admiration for, and later friendship with, the composer Anton Bruckner, who was then in his early fifties and making a precarious living from teaching at the Vienna Conservatory (and later also at the university). Bruckner's reputation as a composer was at a low ebb, and he clearly appreciated the support and encouragement of these lively, talented young men. In later years Mahler was keen to stress that Bruckner was not one of his official teachers. He did, however, attend some of Bruckner's university lectures, and in a letter to Bruckner's first biographer, August Göllerich, admitted to feeling deeply indebted to the older composer:

I was never one of Bruckner's pupils. People say that I was because I could often be seen with him and, in any case, I was one of his particular admirers and supporters. I even believe that at that time I was, together with my friend Krzyzanowski... the only one. I think this was during the years 1875 to 1881... My contact with him lasted until the completion of his Seventh Symphony. I can still remember with pleasure how one morning, during a lecture at the university, he called me out of the lecture theatre (to the astonishment of my colleagues) and played the wonderful theme of the Adagio to me on a very dusty piano: you know yourself what Bruckner

*was like. He had an untainted happiness, which at that
time was youthful, almost childlike, as well as an inherently
trusting nature. Thus despite the large gap between us, we had
a friendly relationship. It was therefore natural that I should
develop both a knowledge and a recognition of his life and
goals, which in turn did not remain without influence on my
educational development as both an artist and an individual.
And so I may, with more right than most, call myself his 'pupil',
and will always do this in grateful admiration.*

The influence of Bruckner's music can be heard at several
key points in Mahler's symphonies: in the triumphant brass
chorale and ecstatic 'pealing' string scales at the end of the
Fifth Symphony; in the direct quotations from Bruckner by
the clarinet in the scherzo of the Second; or in
the upward-straining violin figures that open the
final *Adagio* of the Ninth (clearly inspired by the
opening of the *Adagio* in Bruckner's own Ninth
Symphony). But it was not simply a matter of
imitating the older master's music. Bruckner's
'almost childlike' Roman Catholic faith left its
imprint on Mahler, who became fascinated by
Catholic mysticism (however many doubts he
may have had about the doctrine). This fascination also seems
to have colored his depiction of the child's view of heaven in
the song-finale of his own Fourth Symphony. Mahler may
never have shared Bruckner's religious convictions (his later
conversion to Roman Catholicism was almost certainly a
political move for professional reasons), although there is
evidence that he saw it as an ideal to which, at times, he could
aspire.

Mahler was able to perform one immensely important
service for Bruckner at the time of what was probably the

> Mahler was able to
> perform one immensely
> important service for
> Bruckner at the time
> of what was probably
> the older composer's
> greatest humiliation.

older composer's greatest humiliation. The first performance of Bruckner's Third Symphony in Vienna in 1877 was a fiasco. The audience left the hall in droves, and the critics were either dismissive or downright savage. Mahler, aged seventeen, was one of the handful of supporters who remained in the hall to cheer the composer at the end, and he happily accepted a commission from the publisher Rättig to arrange the work for piano duet. Bruckner was so grateful that when Mahler's arrangement (possibly with Krzyzanowski's help) was published the following year he gave the manuscript of the symphony's second version to Mahler.

Mahler and his friends Wolf and Krzyzanowski also shared Bruckner's intense devotion to the music of Richard Wagner (1813–1883), then the epitome of 'modernism' in music, and a figure who divided opinion among music lovers everywhere, not least in Vienna. Wagner regarded 'absolute', 'pure' musical forms like the symphony as a cultural aberration, and sought to draw all the arts back together into a grand synthesis that he called the *Gesamtkunstwerk* ('total work of art'), embodied in the new form of 'music drama' or in the literature-inspired 'symphonic poems' of his ally Franz Liszt (1811–1886). Enemies of Wagner's thinking, such as the hugely influential Viennese critic Eduard Hanslick (1825–1904), tended to group themselves around the composer Johannes Brahms (1833–1897), then also resident in Vienna and very much a 'Classical Romantic' concentrating on the 'pure' musical forms that Wagner claimed were now out-of-date. When Bruckner, Mahler and his student friends went to the Vienna Opera, they made a point of standing together in the cheaper parts of the hall, while Brahms sat apart 'in splendid isolation' in a private box. The Wagner–Brahms conflict politicized almost

> The Wagner–Brahms conflict politicized almost every aspect of musical life in Vienna at that time, even down to such issues as how much you paid for your opera tickets. There are records of fights breaking out at concerts between groups of rival supporters.

every aspect of musical life in Vienna at that time, even down to such issues as how much you paid for your opera tickets. There are records of fights breaking out at concerts between groups of rival supporters. Sibelius, studying in Vienna in 1890–1, twisted his ankle badly during one such scuffle at a performance of Bruckner's Third Symphony.

By the time, therefore, that Mahler graduated from the Conservatory in 1878, he had been thoroughly initiated into the ideas and politics of modern music. He had also distinguished himself academically, winning prizes for his performance of a Schubert piano sonata, and for a piano quintet and a scherzo for piano quartet that he composed during his studies (both, alas, now lost). And yet Mahler was no exclusive 'musician's musician'. He went to lectures on philosophy and art history at the university and read widely. He also spent a great deal of time walking and thinking – once remarking, half-humorously, that it was only the Vienna Woods that he attended with any regularity. He now had dreams of becoming a full-time composer but he also had to make a living, which for the moment meant teaching (increasingly an ordeal for the ambitious Mahler). At the same time he was suffering from an infatuation, apparently unrequited, for Josephine Poisl, the daughter of Iglau's Chief Telegrapher. Mahler composed three songs for tenor and piano, which he dedicated to Josephine. These have survived and, while slight in substance, they do show hints of greater things to come: already one can sense Mahler beginning to strain against the limiting expressive conventions of his day.

My Child of Sorrow: Das klagende Lied

In 1880, at the age of twenty, Mahler suddenly produced a work of significance: 'My first work in which I found myself as "Mahler", as he later put it. This was the choral-orchestral cantata *Das klagende Lied* (*The Song of Sorrow*); later Mahler was to refer to it as his 'child of sorrow'. Perhaps the frustrations of the Josephine Poisl episode made an impression on the music, but there is stronger evidence that the death of his brother Ernst haunted Mahler as he worked on this: the folk-based story tells of how a young man murders his brother as they compete for the hand of a 'proud queen'. The name 'Ernst' is scrawled on Mahler's manuscript at several key points. It is not clear why Mahler should have been so stirred by a mythical account of fratricide, unless this is an example of what psychologists call 'survivor guilt'.

When Mahler later revised *Das klagende Lied* he omitted the first of the three parts, 'Wäldmärchen' ('Forest Legend'), leaving just two sections: 'Der Spielmann' ('The Minstrel') and 'Hochzeitsstück' ('Wedding Music'). In some ways the decision makes sense. 'Wäldmärchen' is by far the longest and most diffuse of the three sections, and excising it removes a dramatic tautology (the story of the murder being retold at some length in 'Der Spielmann'); it is, however, a shame to lose the magical woodland music that Mahler creates in 'Wäldmärchen' – and also the manner in which he carefully establishes the significant motifs in that original first section.

As a whole, whether in its two- or three-part form, *Das klagende Lied* is inconsistent in quality (the choral writing in particular can be a bit four-square), but it contains more than just flashes of the mature Mahler. So much of his utterly distinctive sound-world is already here, and not just in mere embryo. In 1893, while he was revising *Das klagende Lied*, Mahler wrote to Natalie Bauer-Lechner:

...all the 'Mahler' whom you know was here revealed at one single stroke. What surprises me most is that even

*in the instrumentation nothing has to be altered, it is so
characteristic and new... I cannot understand how so strange
and powerful a work could have come from the pen of a young
man of twenty.*

It is 'characteristic' indeed. The nature music in *Das klagende
Lied* already has the quasi-mystical 'absorbed' quality that is
found in many of the later songs and symphonies. The funeral
march at the beginning of 'Der Spielmann' is pure Mahler
while the sudden brutal *fortissimo* A minor
chord at the work's end (after a long, poignant
dying away) looks forward directly to the end
of the Sixth Symphony. Also typical of the later
works are the sharply distinct orchestral colors,
at times more like spices in an oriental dish than
the richly blended orchestral gravy of Brahms.
Then there is the characteristic juxtaposition
of tragedy with macabre mockery, plus the
sustained nervous intensity (plenty of harsh jabs,
sudden changes of dynamic and nervous string tremolos).
The highly theatrical use of an offstage band to illustrate
the wedding revelry anticipates similar spatial effects in the
Second, Third, Sixth and Eighth symphonies.

all the 'Mahler' whom you
know was here revealed
at one single stroke. I
cannot understand how
so strange and powerful
a work could have come
from the pen of a young
man of twenty.

Wagner may have turned his back on 'absolute' music, but
in *Das klagende Lied* the young modernist Mahler finds in
a hybrid musical form the beginning of a path back to the
symphony: a new kind of symphony in which abstract thematic
development combines with the storytelling innovations of
the Lisztian symphonic poem. 'Sorrow' had helped Mahler
find his true voice, just as it would so often in his later works.

Full of pride in his achievement, Mahler entered *Das
klagende Lied* for the Vienna Conservatory's Beethoven
Prize in 1881 (the jury included Brahms, the conductor

Hans Richter and the composer Carl Goldmark). It was emphatically rejected. Exactly why is not easy to gauge: perhaps the sheer ambitiousness of Mahler's conception weighed against him; or perhaps the grim subject matter, and the intensity with which some of it is expressed, made the judges uncomfortable. Mahler later complained that if he had won the prize he would never have been forced to take up conducting. That is not likely to have been the case – but, either way, Mahler now needed to make his own living, and to find the means to do so.

Chapter 2
The Wanderer

The Wanderer

By 1881 Mahler's first extended period in Vienna was nearing its end. It was to be followed by about a decade and a half of wandering, as Mahler sought to balance his need to generate income with the equally pressing need for artistic fulfilment. During this period his compositions were surprisingly few and far between. After the experience of 'finding himself as "Mahler"', in *Das klagende Lied*, he might have been expected to follow it quickly with more giant steps forward. In fact, it was to be another four years before he completed his next important work: the relatively short but fully mature song cycle *Lieder eines fahrenden Gesellen* ('Songs of a Wayfarer'). Part of the problem was that the conflict between composing and his chosen profession of conducting was not simply a matter of creativity versus the need to make money. As he progressed, Mahler found conducting more and more artistically satisfying in its own right: satisfying but also creatively demanding. Today Mahler is remembered as a composer who also conducted, but in his own day – at least until his final years – he came to be seen as an outstanding conductor who also composed (to which some would have added 'unfortunately'). When Alma Mahler, in *Memories and Letters*, describes her first encounters with her future husband, she makes it clear that while his performances as a conductor of opera were widely lauded his own music was often dismissed. Alma remembers her stepfather Carl Moll telling her, 'they say it's no go.' It was clearly very difficult for Mahler to find time and energy for composing, particularly without encouragement from friends and colleagues.

'A Bogus Goethe'

One other important influence from Mahler's early Viennese years was the young poet and dramatist Siegfried Lipiner (1863–1911), a fellow Jew from the Eastern European province of Galicia (then part of Austria, now belonging to the Ukraine) and an intellectual prodigy. He had the support both of Wagner and the philosopher Friedrich Nietzsche (1844–1900), and probably played an important role in introducing Mahler to Nietzsche's thought. By all accounts Lipiner was mesmerizing, extraordinarily eloquent and very ugly. Alma Mahler has little good to say about him in *Memories and Letters*, but she seems to have disliked nearly all Mahler's close acquaintances, particularly those from his earlier years. 'His friends could never be friends of mine,' she tells us bluntly. Later, she provides an extended portrait of Lipiner, etched with acid:

> *Siegfried Lipiner was undoubtedly a very clever man, an all-round scholar without a single idea of his own. Even in conversation he always brought quotations to his aid in order to make anything clear; he never had anything of his own to say. He may have had originality in his youth; if so, that spring had prematurely dried up. Nietzsche had hopes of him; Wagner too. But his surviving work is eclectic in nature and turgid in manner. He was an ill-natured, harsh-tempered brute. His eyes were much too close together and surmounted*

by an enormous bald skull. He had a stammer, he was a bogus
Goethe in his writing and a haggling Jew in his talk. Mahler
was always overcome by his stupendous knowledge.

In the climate of the time, such racist remarks as 'haggling Jew' were too commonplace to merit explanation, and even the wife of a great Jewish musician could introduce them quite casually into her writing. In passing, and probably unintentionally, Alma gives a clear idea of the attitudes with which Mahler habitually had to contend.

Posterity has not been much kinder to Lipiner's work than Alma was, but the effect of his conversation on Mahler was enormous and at least partly beneficial, which may go some way to explaining Alma's resentment of him. In later years Mahler developed an ambiguous attitude to such Lipiner favorites as Nietzsche and the earlier German philosopher Arthur Schopenhauer (1788–1860), the latter a seminal influence on Wagner's thinking. Both nevertheless remained important points of reference for Mahler, especially Nietzsche, whose writings he both invokes and sets to music in his Third Symphony, and which may also have affected his ideas about tragedy when he came to write his Sixth Symphony (which briefly carried the title 'Tragic').

Mounting the Podium: First Steps

It does not appear to have been Lipiner who pointed Mahler in the direction of conducting as a profession. Realizing that he could not support himself simply by teaching, Mahler made a shrewd move and found himself an agent, Gustav Levy, in 1880. Levy found him something quite quickly, though it hardly looked promising: a job conducting operetta at the provincial Austrian spa town of Bad Hall. Mahler was not enthusiastic, but his Conservatory tutor Julius Epstein encouraged him to take it, with the prophetic words, 'you'll very soon work your way up'. The Bad Hall experience was, on the whole, pretty grim. Mahler found himself conducting scraps of the frothiest Viennese operettas, a repertoire for which he would have mixed feelings in later life. Not only that, but he had no practical assistance, so he found himself also expected to set out music stands for the tiny orchestra as well as chairs for the guests. Conducting indifferent music, with a barely adequate band, to audiences of elderly, frequently somnolent convalescents was hardly an auspicious start, but it did not put Mahler off conducting as a possible 'day job'. When Levy made his next offer – a more permanent and respectable conducting post in Laibach (now Ljubljana, capital of Slovenia) – Mahler agreed to fill the vacancy.

Conditions at the Laibach Landestheater were a significant improvement on Bad Hall. Although the forces at Mahler's disposal were still extraordinarily small by modern standards (an orchestra of eighteen and a chorus of fourteen), Mahler could now try his hand at more serious operatic repertoire, and no longer in 'bleeding chunks'. Anecdotes exist of Mahler being required to perform all manner of heroics to save performances, even singing or whistling from the pit to make up for missing singers. Nevertheless, Laibach had a fairly good reputation at that time. Mahler only stayed there from September 1881 to the following March, but the reviews were good, and when he left he was given a special benefit concert and presented with a laurel wreath. He showed plenty of his father's drive and ruthless determination there, and may have bruised a few delicate egos along the way, but his results were evidently appreciated.

> Conducting indifferent music, with a barely adequate band, to audiences of elderly, frequently somnolent convalescents was hardly an auspicious start, but it did not put Mahler off conducting as a possible 'day job'.

Mahler spent the first three months of 1883 conducting opera in Olmütz (now Olomouc) in Moravia. His verdict on this episode was caustic: 'When you harness a noble steed to a cart drawn by oxen, all it can do is sweat and drag it along with them.' Yet again, he is reported to have achieved striking results with unpromising resources. A baritone in the company, Jacques Manheit (to whom Mahler made the above-quoted remark), remembered Mahler as a dictator, but a dictator whom it was difficult not to admire:

> He was not liked, but they learned to fear him. His manner of demanding and commanding was so decisive that no one dared oppose him, especially since performances had greatly improved under his direction. He hardly knew a single opera, learning each work as he went along. He did not mind that no one sought his company; all he demanded was that each did his duty. I considered myself lucky to see him often.

Manheit tells another story that gives an intriguing insight into Mahler's sense of personal priority at that time:

> The following episode is highly characteristic. One day I found Mahler in the café, utterly self-absorbed. When I asked why he was so sad, he replied that he had received bad news from home, his father was ill. Next morning on my way to the theatre I saw a man running demented, weeping loudly, through the streets. With some difficulty, I recognised Mahler. Remembering the previous day's events, I asked anxiously, 'In heaven's name, has something happened to your father?' 'Worse, worse, much worse,' howled Mahler. 'The worst has happened. The Master has died!' It was 13 February 1883. Richard Wagner had been taken from us. It was impossible to talk to Mahler for days afterwards. He came to rehearsals and performances, but remained inaccessible to everyone for

a long time.

Soon afterwards Mahler made his first pilgrimage to the Festspielhaus, Bayreuth, to hear Wagner's culminating masterwork, the 'sacred stage drama' *Parsifal*. Wagner had forbidden performances in all but his own, specially built opera house. The experience left a deep impression on Mahler, and no doubt raised his hopes about what could be achieved in the opera house, especially in the cause of his revered 'Master'.

While Mahler was in Olmütz, a senior stage director from the Dresden Court Opera, Karl Überhorst, heard him conducting *Joseph*, by the French composer Étienne-Nicolas Méhul. 'A man who can bring off a performance like that is something astonishing,' he exclaimed; but Überhorst baulked at Mahler's personal appearance and, instead of putting forward his name at Dresden, recommended him to a colleague in the Prussian city of Kassel. Mahler was engaged that same year.

Mahler in 1884

He now had bigger and better forces to command. Ultimate control of the opera house, however, was in the hands of another strong-willed dictator, the resonantly named general manager Adolph Freiherr [Baron] von und zu Gilsa, a veteran soldier and proud bearer of the Iron Cross.

There was a clash of wills and, humiliatingly, the ambitious Mahler found himself second in command as conductor to the solidly capable Wilhelm Treibner, also Court Kapellmeister, who insisted on keeping the best repertoire for himself. Again the public and critical response to Mahler's conducting was very good, but the singers and orchestral players were frequently provoked to fury. After one particularly tense rehearsal, so the story goes, some of the musicians turned up armed with cudgels.

Bristling with frustration, Mahler fired off job applications in all directions. Then, suddenly, he was rewarded with two offers: the conductor's post at the Leipzig Municipal Theatre from mid-1886, and an interim appointment at the Deutsche Landestheater in Prague. Before he left Kassel, Mahler was involved in a truly titanic clash with Treibner over who was to direct a prestigious performance of Mendelssohn's oratorio *St Paul* at a big gala concert, with a 400-strong choir and a top-rank orchestra. Mahler's success in Kassel gave him the political leverage he needed, and in the end Treibner had to be content with rehearsing the orchestra. However, this gave Mahler his first taste of public anti-Semitism: one local newspaper reported that 'the Germans do the work and the Jew gets the honor'. Scared by this opprobrium, the orchestra pulled out of the concert but Mahler refused to be beaten. Using his own financial resources and enormous powers of persuasion, he simply recruited his own orchestra. The concert went ahead and, despite the best efforts of the press, it was a huge success.

> Again the public and critical response to Mahler's conducting was very good, but the singers and orchestral players were frequently provoked to fury. After one particularly tense rehearsal, so the story goes, some of the musicians turned up armed with cudgels.

'Two Blue Eyes': Lieder eines fahrenden Gesellen

There were other, more private emotional storms for Mahler during his stay at Kassel. Among the cast of singers was an attractive, blue-eyed singer named Johanna Richter, with whom Mahler fell passionately in love; this time his feelings do appear to have been reciprocated. Predictably, it all ended in tears, but the Johanna affair was artistically more productive than his earlier unhappy infatuation with Josephine Poisl. Mahler put together six poems for Johanna. Although these were heavily indebted to *Des Knaben Wunderhorn* ('The Boy's Magic Horn'), the collection of German folk poetry assembled by Achim von Arnim and Clemens Brentano in the early nineteenth century, Mahler's adaptations and additions are skilful and entirely idiomatic. More importantly, four of them became the basis of his first great song cycle *Lieder eines fahrenden Gesellen* ('Songs of a Wayfarer'), composed in 1884 but not performed publicly until 1896.

In *Lieder eines fahrenden Gesellen*, Mahler the self-dramatizer steps forward as never before. The mood-swings of a passionate love affair, from ecstasy to despondency, are recorded vividly, and with that very personal intensity so typical of Mahler. But at the same time he is acutely conscious of artistic lineage. In *Lieder eines fahrenden Gesellen* Mahler – he who was dubbed 'another Schubert' – does not simply imitate this master of song, he evokes him and his emotional world in order to emphasize his chosen self-image as the suffering romantic 'Wanderer'. There are obvious echoes, in text and music, of Schubert's *Winterreise* and *Die schöne Müllerin* ('The Miller's Beautiful Daughter'). As in both Schubert cycles, the outcast lover goes on a journey that leads away from the promise of happiness in love to final hope of relief in death. Schubert's imagery is echoed too. Even the linden tree that stirs up such powerful mixed feelings in the first part of *Winterreise* returns in the final song of *Lieder eines fahrenden Gesellen*, as the lover's grief finds final release. At the same time, Mahler seems to stamp the particulars of his own experience on the work: the beloved girl has 'blue eyes', just like Johanna.

Even more than *Das klagende Lied*, *Lieder eines fahrenden Gesellen* is brim-full of characteristic Mahlerian colors and devices. The very first sounds are a classic demonstration of his much-celebrated irony. Lightly dancing, folk-like figures on clarinets and a tinkling triangle are set in a dark, minor mode, suggesting simultaneously the happiness of the beloved's wedding music and the dejection of the jilted lover, standing outside. The second song, 'Ging heut' Morgen übers Feld' ('I went this morning over the fields'), starts with the image of the happy wanderer, delighting in nature (as at the beginning of Schubert's *Die schöne Müllerin*), but ends with a typical Mahlerian reversal: 'Will my happiness blossom again like the spring? No, it will never blossom again.' Then comes 'Ich hab' ein glühend Messer' ('I have a burning knife') – stormy, with brilliant, acrid orchestration portraying the knife-stabs of pain in the wayfarer's heart. Finally comes the most Schubertian movement of all: **'Die zwei blauen Augen von meinem Schatz'** ('My darling's two blue eyes'). This is a slow, sad, funereal march, downcast rather than ceremonial, full of the kind of poignant major–minor alternations beloved of Schubert, but which Mahler was able to make so much his own. The most telling moment comes at the very end. As the boy dreams of peaceful oblivion under the linden tree, the mode changes to a comforting major, with soft muted horns and gently undulating harp; then, for just two bars, flutes and harp bring back the minor-key funereal motif, and hope is extinguished as softly as a snuffed-out candle. Years later, in his influential study *Musicians of Today*, the French novelist and writer on music

Romain Rolland (not an unqualified admirer of Mahler) made this perceptive observation: 'perhaps no one is nearer the secret of Schubert's moving and voluptuous melancholy.' Of no Mahler work is this truer than the *Lieder eines fahrenden Gesellen.*

New Triumphs; New Disasters

Whatever the ultimate fate of Mahler's wayfarer, for Mahler himself the journey went on, and this meant the planned move from Kassel to Prague. Once again, Mahler enjoyed a number of triumphs, even though the German Landestheater was being upstaged by the rival Czech National Theatre (nationalism was very much on the rise here, as throughout the Austrian Empire). The Prague stay had been planned as a stopgap, but Mahler came to like it so much that he tried to stay on. Here, too, he was able to stage a performance of three of his own songs; not outstandingly successful, it was nonetheless a useful learning experience.

Then, in August 1886, came the move to Leipzig. Mahler was once more in a junior position, as second conductor to Arthur Nikisch (1855–1922), only five years older than Mahler but already a big name and very much the star attraction in Leipzig. One can imagine Mahler's feelings about that. This time, however, he was allowed to conduct major repertoire, including, at last, Wagner. Luckily for Mahler, less so for Nikisch, the latter contracted pneumonia and the 'assistant' had to step in and conduct a complete performance of Wagner's opera cycle *Der Ring des Nibelungen* ('The Ring of the Nibelung'). After this he went from success to success, although one or two critics took him to task for his relatively free attitude to tempo; this was to be a recurring complaint throughout Mahler's career, especially when he conducted the music of Beethoven and Mozart.

Mahler at this time became involved in another intense and hopelessly tangled love affair. This time the object of his affections was an older woman, Marion von Weber, whose husband Carl was the grandson of Carl Maria von Weber (1786–1826), composer of the masterpiece of German Romantic opera, *Der Freischütz* ('The Free-shooter'). Carl von Weber, a captain in the Leipzig Regiment, invited Mahler to assist in completing a comic opera that his grandfather had left in fragmentary form: *Die drei Pintos* ('The Three Pintos'). Mahler's completion was highly successful, and was soon taken up by other opera houses. This was gratifying for Mahler on one level, although it was still some way from the success that he most deeply craved as a composer in his own right.

Working in the Weber household was a great source of pleasure for Mahler: he called it his 'escape hatch from the world'. The Webers gave him much-needed encouragement in his composing efforts, too; and Mahler played parts of his new First Symphony to them as he wrote it. But soon it was Marion who was the real focus of his devotion. Alas, the word 'discretion' was not in Mahler's vocabulary, and soon a scandal erupted. The British composer and pioneering suffragette Ethel Smyth was in Leipzig at the time the Mahler–Weber affair became public, and she left a vivid account of its fallout, plus a valuable portrait of Mahler as man and conductor:

> *The poor Webers' subsequent history was tragic. Gustav Mahler, who was then one of the conductors at the Leipzig Opera, fell in love with [Marion] and his passion was reciprocated, as well it might be, for in spite of his ugliness he had a demoniacal charm. A scandal would mean leaving*

The word 'discretion' was not in Mahler's vocabulary, and soon a scandal erupted.

the army, and Weber shut his eyes to it as long as was possible, but Mahler, a tyrannical lover, never hesitated to compromise his mistresses. Things were getting critical, when one day, travelling to Dresden in the company of strangers, Weber suddenly burst out laughing, drew a revolver, and began taking William Tell-like shots at the head rests between the seats. He was overpowered, the train brought to a standstill, and they took him to the police station raving mad, thence to an asylum. Always considered rather queer in the army, the Mahler business had broken down his brain. I afterwards heard he had lucid intervals, that his wife in an agony of remorse refused to see her lover again... and the rest is silence.

Mahler's life was full of incidents of this sort, and knowing him even as slightly as I did I can well believe it, not being able to conceive that any woman who loved and was loved by him could resist him. I even felt this when I saw him last (it was in Vienna in 1907), worn out, exasperated, prematurely aged, wrestling with the Habsburgs as personified by the Intendant of the Opera House he had made the first in the world. He was far and away the finest conductor I ever knew, with the most all-embracing musical instinct, and it is one of the small tragedies of my life that just when he was considering the question of producing [my] The Wreckers *at Vienna they drove him from office. When he was gone even his enemies regretted their action; but the ideal of art he set, his passionate refusal to abate just one jot or tittle of his artistic demands, the magnitude and purity of his vision, these are things that start a tradition and linger after sunset... At the time I am speaking of in Leipzig I saw but little of him, and we didn't get on; I was too young and raw then to appreciate this grim personality, intercourse with whom was like handling a bomb cased in razor-edges.*

Of the many memorable phrases in Smyth's account, the last, 'a bomb cased in razor-edges', is perhaps the best of all. To those who know Mahler's music it will bring to mind passage after passage in his symphonies and orchestral songs: the lacerating harshness of parts of the Fifth and Sixth symphonies perhaps, or the burning knife-thrusts of 'Ich hab' ein glühend Messer' from *Lieder eines fahrenden Gesellen*. There, as so often, the man and the music are of a piece.

'Titan': The First Symphony

To appreciate how new and difficult Mahler's music must have seemed at the time, it is worth remembering that when he began his First Symphony in 1884, 'modern music' meant Wagner. That great musical revolutionary had brought new ambiguity to the long-established tonal language, and exploited the potential of the unresolved dissonance to suggest unappeasable erotic longing in his great music drama *Tristan und Isolde*. The Wagnerian revolution was largely confined, however, to opera and the Lisztian symphonic poem, and the standard by which new symphonies were judged was still that of Brahms. In a Brahmsian symphony there was little room for Wagner's highly charged harmonic ambiguity or seductive new orchestral colors (still less for literary programmes). Brahms's symphony was a 'pure' form, proudly indebted to the earlier Viennese masters in its use of form and expressive language. Indeed, the orchestral forces employed by Brahms were essentially the same as those in Beethoven's and Schubert's symphonies, three-quarters of a century earlier.

For audiences brought up on Brahms, therefore, hearing Mahler's First Symphony would have been like stepping into a new world. The opening can surprise even today: one note, an A, is spread through almost the entire range of the string section, topped with ghostly violin harmonics. Other unusual colors follow: distant trumpet fanfares (surely echoes of the military music from Mahler's childhood), high clarinet cuckoo-calls, a plaintive cor anglais, the bell-like bass notes of the harp. All this would have been startlingly new in Mahler's time – and yet there is nothing tentative or experimental about this symphonic debut. Just as in *Das klagende Lied* and *Lieder eines fahrenden Gesellen*, Mahler knows precisely

> For audiences brought up on Brahms hearing Mahler's First Symphony would have been like stepping into a new world. The opening can surprise even today

the sound he wants, and precisely how to get it. His experience in the theatre pit, coaxing great music out of sometimes indifferent musicians, in immensely variable acoustics, tells in every bar of the First Symphony's wonderfully atmospheric slow introduction.

Still, there is much more to Mahler's First Symphony than innovative orchestral colors and theatrical sound effects. When the symphony was first performed in 1889 it bore a title, 'Titan', taken from the once-famous novel by the German Romantic writer Jean Paul (the pen name of Johann Paul Richter, 1763–1825). Richter's *Titan* tells of two 'titanic' men: geniuses or, as the author calls them, *Himmelstürmer* ('Heaven-stormers'). The first is devoted to freedom of thought, the other to hedonism, but they are ultimately balanced by a third character, Albano, who reconciles their extremes. There are prophetic echoes here of Nietzsche's ideal of the *Übermensch* ('Superman') who marries 'Apollonian' love of order and form with 'Dionysian' extremism. One can understand the emotionally effusive style of Richter's novel appealing to Mahler; it also includes some very beautiful evocations of landscape, especially by night – again a very Mahlerian theme.

For the First Symphony's premiere, Mahler set out his version of the 'Titan' theme in an explanatory programme note. This tells how the symphony progresses from 'the awakening of nature at early dawn', through youthful happiness and love, to the sardonic gloom of the funeral march, and then to the finale, subtitled 'From Inferno to Paradise'. It was clear that Mahler's interest in Richter's novel was more than literary. Its description of the pains of a love affair that ends tragically evidently impressed Mahler. Behind the symphony, he hinted to friends, was the memory of a love affair that had ended, painfully, at about the time he began writing the work. Whether he is here referring to Johanna Richter or Marion von Weber is not immediately obvious, but there are clues in the very fabric of the symphony, placed with a characteristically deft yet enigmatic hand.

Before long, however, Mahler began to have doubts about literary programmes, this one included. In 1896 he wrote to his friend, the sympathetic critic Max Marschalk. His explanation reads like a precarious intellectual balancing-act:

I would like it stressed that the symphony is greater than the love affair it is based on, or rather it preceded it as far as the emotional life of the creator is concerned. The real affair became the reason for, but by no means the real meaning of, the work... My need to express my feelings in music in a symphony begins only where the mysterious feelings take over at the gate which leads into the 'other world', a world which does not separate happenings through time or space. Just as I find it a platitude to invent music to fit a programme, I find it sterile to give a programme for a completed work. The fact that the inspiration or basis of a composition is an experience of its author does not alter things.

In later life Mahler could be blunt on this subject: when someone once raised the issue at an evening drinks party, Mahler is said to have leapt to his feet, emptied his glass, and shouted, 'Perish all programmes!' Most listeners find that this music, so overflowing with passion, drama and the sounds of nature, cannot be fully explained in the detached terms of musical analysis alone. Yet, whatever Mahler may have felt about explicit written programmes, the First Symphony is full of pointers to possible meanings beyond the notes. The main theme of the first movement, heard on cellos and basses after the slow, intensely atmospheric 'dawn' introduction, is taken straight from the second of the earlier *Lieder eines fahrenden Gesellen*, written, Mahler later confessed, as a 'memorial' to his affair with Johanna Richter. (Johanna was no relation of Richter the novelist, but the name connection is striking.) That song concerned a young man, jilted in love, setting out on a beautiful spring morning, hoping that nature will help his own heart to heal. For most of the first movement, Mahler seems to share the young man's hope. Then, however, there comes a darkly mysterious passage, echoing the 'dawn' introduction, but adding sinister new sounds – the low, quiet growl of a tuba, ominous drum-beats and a repeated sighing figure for cellos. For a moment, the music seems to echo the final words of the song: 'Will my happiness blossom again like the spring? No, it will never blossom again.'

When the First Symphony had its initial performances, an extra movement followed the first: a short, song-like *Andante* led by a sweet trumpet melody. Carrying the title 'Blumine', it derives from music Mahler wrote earlier (and which was either lost or destroyed) for Joseph Scheffel's half-sentimental, half-humorous play *Der Trompeter von Säckingen* ('The Trumpeter of Säckingen'). In the play, the music illustrates 'a moonlight serenade on the trumpet blown across the Rhine'.

Critics still argue about whether Mahler was right to remove this movement from the symphony. Certainly it makes the work longer, but it contains an important anticipation of the finale's ardently lyrical second theme; with *Blumine* restored, that impassioned final theme acquires the extra significance of a reminiscence. Mahler wrote his *Der Trompeter von Säckingen* music in 1884, while he was still working at Kassel (indicating another possible connection with Johanna).

Dance music dominates the next movement, the symphony's **scherzo**, especially the robust, earthy vigor of the Austrian Ländler (the country cousin of the sophisticated urban waltz). There are hints here of another, earlier song, *Hans und Grethe* (apparently one of the three performed in Prague), in which gawky young Hans finds a sweetheart at a village dance; it is all innocent happiness. The slower, more reflective trio brings adult expression: nostalgia and, later, sarcasm (shrill high woodwind). After this comes complete contrast in the form of an eerie, sardonic funeral march, partly inspired by a painting by Jacques Callot, *The Huntsman's Funeral*, in which a procession of animals carries the hunter to his grave. One by one, the orchestral instruments enter quietly, playing a famous old nursery tune, *Frère Jacques*, or, as Mahler would have known it, 'Bruder Martin, schläfst du?' ('Brother Martin, are you sleeping?'). The movement's most significant section features a lengthy quotation from the final song of the *Lieder eines fahrenden Gesellen* – at the point when the grief-stricken young man who has lost his beloved finds consolation in the thought of death. This is without a doubt the dark heart of the First Symphony.

Nor is this the end of the story. In the finale Mahler strives onwards, in the words of the discarded programme, from 'Inferno to Paradise'. At first all is turbulence, but when the storm has died down, strings present the ardent, slower melody, which is unmistakably a love theme. There is a brief memory of the first movement's 'dawn' music, then the struggle begins again. Eventually massed horns introduce a new, radiantly hopeful theme, strongly reminiscent of 'And he shall reign' from Handel's *Messiah*. Mahler gives an idea of a possible 'higher' kind of programme at this point in a letter to a new friend that he made while he was writing the First Symphony: the brilliant and successful young composer and conductor Richard Strauss (1864–1949). Strauss was perplexed by what appeared to be the symphony's premature triumph at this stage. Mahler explained:

> At the place in question the conclusion is merely apparent (in the full sense of a 'false conclusion'), and a change and breaking-down that reaches to the essence is needed before a true 'victory' can be won after such a struggle. My intention was to show a struggle in which victory is furthest from the protagonist just when he believes it closest. This is the nature of every spiritual *struggle*. For it is by no means so simple to become or to be a hero.

The 'breaking-down' is followed by more reminiscences, beginning with a still more direct reference to the symphony's original 'dawn' music. Heroic struggles recommence, until dark introspection is finally overcome, and the symphony ends in jubilation, with 'And he shall reign' now clad in even greater orchestral splendor. Mahler's hero has survived, like the composer himself, to live, and love, another day.

> My intention was to show a struggle in which victory is furthest from the protagonist just when he believes it closest. This is the nature of every spiritual struggle. For it is by no means so simple to become or to be a hero.

43

Chapter 3

Resurrection

Resurrection

As Mahler approached his thirtieth birthday in 1890, taking stock of his career thus far, he probably felt a mixture of hope and frustration. He had completed a major song cycle (*Lieder eines fahrenden Gesellen*) and composed his first symphony. He had also begun the series of settings of poems from the great folk collection *Des Knaben Wunderhorn* – strong and characterful songs that provide valuable pointers to possible 'meanings' in the symphonies. The Second, Third and Fourth symphonies are indeed often labelled the 'Wunderhorn' symphonies because of their close musical relationships to the songs.

Songs without Words

Those first achievements were impressive enough in themselves, but Mahler had had much less success in getting public attention and, more importantly, understanding for his music. There had been very few performances of his works, and when Mahler finally engineered the opportunity to conduct his own First Symphony, in 1889, the result was far from the success with audiences and critics that he yearned for. Still, with the satisfaction of completing Symphony No. 1 still fresh, Mahler turned again to thoughts of large-scale composition; the question was what kind of large-scale composition it should be. For many Wagnerian modernists, the abstract medium of the symphony was no longer an option, while those who still believed that it was the right form to convey the loftiest musical thoughts tended to fall into the Brahmsian conservative camp and were thus suspicious of any attempts to introduce programmes or other extra-musical elements. There must have been times when Mahler wondered if he was not in danger of falling between two gigantic ideological stools.

Evidence of such perplexity can be found on the very title page of the next major work that Mahler began. In September 1888 he completed a big, single-movement orchestral work. On the manuscript's first page the words 'Symphony in C minor' are visible, but they have been crossed out and substituted by a title: *Todtenfeier* ('Funeral Rites'). The title echoes the use of funeral marches in the First Symphony and *Lieder eines fahrenden Gesellen*, but while those were only passing details in a larger, richer canvas, here it is the death march that sets the tone and dominates the musical picture. In 1891 Mahler offered this huge single movement to a publisher as a 'symphonic poem' (it was rejected), suggesting that, at this stage, he had abandoned the notion of adding further movements. Perhaps he had even decided that it was time to ditch the symphony as a form altogether and align himself completely with what was then thought to be the 'progressive' camp.

Almost certainly a crucial influence here was his growing friendship (not unmixed with rivalry) with the great rising star of new German music, Richard Strauss. Strauss was four years younger than Mahler, but already the modernist-inclined critics were describing him as the most important composer in the German-speaking world after Wagner. This may well have been galling to Mahler, whose apparently see-sawing estimation of Strauss and his music in later years must to some extent have stemmed from professional jealousy. It was striking, though, that Strauss had achieved his greatest successes in the form of the orchestral symphonic poem: notably with *Don Juan* in 1888 and *Tod und Verklärung* ('Death and Transfiguration') in 1888–9. If Mahler in the late 1880s therefore thought that Wagner was right after all, it may be that the growing success of his old friend and mentor Bruckner in the early 1890s acted as a counterweight. Despite being devoted to Wagner, Bruckner had carried on writing symphonies on something like the old Classical model, and it was with these works that he had begun to convince the Wagnerian progressives that a reconciliation between Wagner's innovations and the tradition-conscious medium of the post-Beethovenian symphony was not only possible but might also point to ways ahead. Whatever the case, Mahler did eventually abandon the idea of issuing *Todtenfeier* as a symphonic poem; the (probably) older scheme of making it the first movement of a vast, multi-movement 'Symphony in C minor' was resurrected, and work began again.

Head of the Family

Mahler had begun this ambitious new symphony with thoughts of death. These must have been intensified by events in 1889, the year after he began the symphony. First, on 18 February 1889, Mahler's father, Bernhard, died; his mother Marie followed on 11 October (she may have been more devoted to her husband than Mahler would have us believe); and not long after that, his sister Leopoldine ('Poldi') died of a brain tumour. Mahler agonized over the 'meaning' of life and death in his various writings on the Second Symphony, and such issues must have had special urgency for him as he was writing the later movements.

In practical terms, Mahler was now the head of the family, responsible for two younger brothers and two sisters, including 'Justi', who remained close to him and kept house for him for a while. All this was a huge financial drain for Mahler, even when his earnings began to improve with his growing status as a conductor. One of his brothers, Alois, was a particular source of concern, eternally prone to financial troubles of one kind or another. Mahler more than ever needed to make as much money as he could from conducting. No wonder he complained repeatedly of being 'on the treadmill', and of having desperately little time for composing.

'On the Treadmill': Hamburg and Budapest

With all that in mind, it is easy to forgive Mahler his occasional resentment of his friend Strauss's success, as composer as well as conductor, and particularly his carping comments about Strauss's alleged 'commercial' attitudes. However, as Mahler was completing *Todtenfeier*, his own fortunes as a conductor were about to take another turn for the better. In 1888 Mahler was at last able to take charge of a major opera house, in the Hungarian capital, Budapest. Since the establishment of the Austro-Hungarian 'dual crown', Hungarian nationalism had been growing: clearly Franz Joseph's attempts to placate the independence movement had only had limited success. Hungarian national feeling affected the opera house too, and Mahler was told to recruit singers as far as possible from Italy and Hungary rather than Germany or Austria. Mahler

In 1888 Mahler was at last able to take charge of a major opera house, in the Hungarian capital, Budapest.

49

was able to make this work to his advantage. When he arrived in Budapest the opera house was significantly in debt, but by refusing to employ expensive German and Austrian star singers and fostering home-grown, less established talent, he was able to make big reductions in the company's overheads and pull it back into the black. This, almost as much as his artistic triumphs, made a very positive impression, and not just in Hungary.

It was Mahler's conducting that drew the most acclaim. The critics were often ecstatic and in 1889 praise came from a very welcome source. Brahms, still the great Classical Romantic, and by no means sympathetic to Mahler's 'modernist' musical instincts, heard Mahler's performance of Mozart's *Don Giovanni* and was hugely impressed. It was the beginning of a very useful relationship for Mahler, even though their views on music's future were so opposed. Brahms's influence on Mahler's behalf was considerable, and his support carried a great deal of weight when Mahler was later angling for the post of Kapellmeister at the Vienna Opera.

Offset against this professional triumph was a galling artistic failure: the premiere of the First Symphony (then entitled 'symphonic poem') in November 1889 was a disaster with both the audience and the critics. Even for more sophisticated musical audiences, Mahler's music was still much too new, especially in its expressive extremes, and its startling use of irony or blatant sarcasm; and his inability to fit into any of the ideological camps then prevalent did not help. His manner – intense, emotionally convulsive, full of ironies, riddles and contradictions – was not easy to 'place'. It would be years before Mahler's language began to be understood by more than a few isolated individuals.

Before long there were problems at Budapest. In 1891 a

new director was appointed at the opera house: Count Géza Zichy. Zichy was a rabid ultra-nationalist who wanted an all-Hungarian opera theatre. He ran what amounted to a campaign of intimidation against Mahler (who on one occasion was actually locked out of the building), and eventually Mahler felt obliged to resign, although this time he was able to arrange a rather handsome pay-off. In any case, a still more tempting offer had arrived from Bernhard Pollini, director of the Hamburg Stadttheater. Mahler was to be First Kapellmeister, with a finer team of singers than he had worked with before. On the downside, major artistic decisions were not to be his responsibility, rehearsal time was inadequate, sets and costumes were shabby, and his workload was immense: as many as 150 performances per season. Mahler also soon formed the opinion, not without justification, that Pollini was more interested in balancing the books than achieving artistic success. These sustained clashes of interest, on top of a Herculean workload, were immensely draining for Mahler; it was no wonder that it took him until 1894 to complete his Second Symphony.

> As in Budapest, there was praise for Mahler from some very high places.

As in Budapest, there was praise for Mahler from some very high places. Hans von Bülow (1830–1894), widely seen as the high priest of German conductors (Brahms being for many the high priest of German composers), was deeply impressed with Mahler's conducting. Von Bülow called Mahler the 'Pygmalion' of the Hamburg Opera, after the Ancient Greek artist who, according to legend, brought an inanimate statue to life. On the other hand, some of the Hamburg critics began to complain about Mahler's relatively free attitude to tempo and his retouching (mostly re-orchestration) of the classics. Mahler felt he had good reasons and argued his case vigorously. Instruments and orchestra sizes had changed since the days of Beethoven and Mozart,

Mahler while at the Hamburg Opera in 1892; photograph signed with signature and 'Wien, November 1897'

and some textures needed adapting to make important details heard. Unquestionably, Mahler did what he did from the highest of artistic motives, as when later he made his own extensive re-orchestration of the symphonies of Schumann (a composer often criticized for a lack of orchestral sense). Even so, many critics felt that Mahler was distorting sacred texts. Mahler was to last six years in Hamburg, but the sniping of the critics and recurring battles with Pollini made him increasingly determined to go to Vienna. Then considered to have the finest opera house in the world, it was also the city that Mahler still tended to think of as his old home town. At any rate, he might feel a little less alien as a Bohemian Austrian Jew in Austria than he did in Germany.

The Part-time Composer

It was during his Hamburg period that Mahler began to work out a practical *modus vivendi* with regard to composition. As long as he was occupied with the opera season he had precious little time or energy left for more personal creative work, but there was a reasonable break during the summer. In 1893 he began a pattern that was to hold good for the rest of his life: spending almost the entire holiday in the Alps composing. His first summer resort was at Steinbach on the shores of the Attersee in the magnificent Alpine region known as the Salzkammergut. Here he had the opportunity to call regularly on Brahms (who at the time took his vacations in the nearby spa town of Bad Ischl) and enjoy disagreeing with him about the future of music; Brahms was ever pessimistic, Mahler defiantly brimming over with hope.

> In 1893 he began a pattern that was to hold good for the rest of his life: spending almost the entire holiday in the Alps composing.

The scenery itself had an enormously stimulating effect on Mahler's musical imagination, for not only is the area fabulously beautiful, it is also a landscape of dramatic extremes. Amid the Alps he was able to write at a fantastic pace. (In 1906 he allegedly completed the sketch score of his colossal Eighth Symphony in as many weeks, working in the little 'composing hut' that he built for himself near the Alpine village of Maiernigg.) It was at Steinbach that Mahler found the peace and natural inspiration he needed to bring his Second Symphony to its affirmative conclusion: the 'Resurrection' finale that resolves the fatal broodings of the *Todtenfeier* first movement.

Mahler's composing hut near Maiernigg

'Prepare Yourself to Live': The Second Symphony

With the Second Symphony, Mahler's ambition and self-confidence as a composer reached new heights. The huge finale amplifies the already large orchestral forces by the addition of chorus and organ, and by increasing the number of trumpets from four to six and the horns from six to ten: surely a record in German symphonic music. Mahler is not, however, simply interested in sheer volume of sound. As in *Das klagende Lied*, he also makes a highly theatrical use of space: for example, the offstage band (sometimes requiring a second conductor) representing the march of the dead to the throne of God on

Judgement Day, or the quiet but awe-inspiring use of distant solo brass evoking the call of the Last Trumpet.

Even though Mahler had decided that this was to be a symphony and not a 'symphonic poem', there was still the question of how much a composer should tell his audience (something that would vex Mahler for years to come). Like the First Symphony, the Second was provided with a long and detailed programme note at its first performance, setting out the ideas behind the music and the emotions they aroused: a kind of literary 'map' to guide the listener through the often complex musical narrative. Yet even from the start, Mahler was uncomfortable with this. When his young admirer Max Marschalk asked him, in 1896, for a key to the 'meaning' of his Second Symphony, Mahler replied:

> *I would regard my work as having failed completely if I found it necessary to give people like yourself even an indication as to its mood-sequence. In my conception of the work I was in no way concerned with the detailed setting-forth of an* event, *but much rather of a* feeling. *The conceptual basis of the work is spoken out clearly in the words of the final chorus, and the sudden emergence of the contralto solo* [in the fourth movement] *throws an illuminating light on the earlier movements.*

When the Second Symphony was published in 1897, Mahler wrote to another admirer, Arthur Seidl, and was clearly at pains to draw a division between his work and the explicit programme music of Strauss:

> *You hit the nail on the head when you say that my music achieves a programme as the final explanation of feelings and ideas, whereas Strauss's programme is the result of a planned*

quota... When I draft a large-scale composition I invariably reach the point where I have to use the word as a carrier of my musical idea.

Mahler would eventually, in his Fifth, Sixth, Seventh, Ninth and Tenth symphonies, feel able to dispense with both written programme notes and sung texts to explain what he calls his music's 'mood-sequence'. He was rarely capable, however, of talking about his music without invoking poetic and even philosophical images. There are also those self-quotations and other kinds of music reference which seem to demand some sort of extra-musical interpretation – a long way, therefore, from Brahms's supposed 'absolute music'.

Explaining the Music

Mahler was continually trying to explain his music in order to make it understood by its audience. Even as late as 1901 he provided a long programme note on the Second Symphony for the King of Saxony. Around the same time Mahler told Strauss that this programme was 'intended for the naïve reader'; so it comes as something of a jolt to find him telling his future wife Alma in a letter in of the same year that 'actually [the notes] were intended for you in the first place'. Presumably she did not know what Mahler had told Strauss about the programme, or she might not have felt so inclined to preserve it (in Mahler's own handwritten version) in her diary. It is worth quoting this programme note in full, as it offers vivid imagery which at many points seems to parallel something of the music's spiritual essence:

Mahler was continually trying to explain his music in order to make it understood by its audience.

—

First movement. We are standing at the grave of a well-loved man. We contemplate his whole life, his struggles, his sufferings and his intentions on earth. And now, in this solemn and deeply stirring moment, when the confusion and distractions of everyday life are lifted like a hood from our eyes, a voice of awe-inspiring solemnity chills our heart, a voice that, blinded by the mirage of everyday life, we usually ignore: 'What next?' it says. 'What is life and what is death? Will we live on eternally? Is it all an empty dream or do our life and death have a meaning?' And we must answer this question, if we mean to go on living.

The next three movements are conceived as intermezzi.

Second movement: Andante. A blissful moment in the life of the dear departed and a sad recollection of his youth and lost innocence.

Third movement: Scherzo. A spirit of disbelief and negation has seized him. He is bewildered by the bustle of appearances and he loses his perception of childhood and the profound strength that love alone can give. He despairs both of himself and God. The world and life begin to seem unreal. Utter disgust for every form of existence and evolution seizes him in an iron grasp, torments him until he utters a cry of despair.

Fourth movement: 'Urlicht' (alto solo). The stirring words of simple faith sound in his ears: 'I am from God and will return to God! The dear God will give me a light, will light me to eternal, blessed life.'

Fifth movement. It begins with the 'cry of despair'. Once more we are confronted with terrifying questions, and the *atmosphere is the same as at the end of the third movement. The voice of the Caller is heard. The end of every living thing has come, the last judgement is at hand and the horror of the day of days has come upon us. The earth trembles, the graves burst open, the dead arise and march forth in endless procession. The great and the lowly of this earth, kings and beggars, the just and the godless, all press forward: 'an endless procession of shuddering, expectant people'. The cry for mercy and forgiveness sounds fearful in our ears. The wailing becomes gradually more terrible; our senses desert us, all consciousness dies as the Eternal Spirit approaches. The 'Last Trump' sounds; the trumpets of the Apocalypse call out 'to all flesh and all spirit'. In the eerie silence that follows we can just barely make out a distant nightingale, a last tremulous echo of earthly life. The gentle sound of a chorus of saints and heavenly hosts is then heard: 'Rise again, yes, rise again thou wilt!' Then God in all His glory comes into sight. A wondrously mild light strikes us to the heart. All is calm and bliss. And lo: there is no judgement; there are no sinners; no just men; no great and no small; there is no punishment and no reward! A feeling of overwhelming love imbues us with the bliss of knowing and being.*

How many composers today would risk addressing their potential audiences in terms like that? Even in Mahler's day, when extravagant literary programme notes were quite commonplace, there must have been those who shook their heads in disbelief at some of Mahler's claims. Here is a composer who dares to suggest that through the medium of his music 'God in all His glory comes into sight'. No doubt this kind of thing would have hardened the resistance of some as much as it aroused the eager anticipation of others: anticipation which (as Dr. Johnson was fond of pointing out, a century before

Mahler) can be considered more of a burden than a blessing when it comes to experiencing the event itself.

Maybe Mahler came to realize that efforts like the above could be counter-productive. In any case, even with the help of the most carefully worded programmes, the public would insist on getting the wrong end of the stick, even the sympathetic public. Alma Mahler remembered how, on their honeymoon in St Petersburg, Mahler made the acquaintance of a person she describes as 'a beautiful old lady of hysterical tendencies'. Years later, when Mahler was in Russia on his own, this lady sent for him:

> ...telling him that she felt her death to be near, and would he enlighten her about the other world, as he had said so much about it in his Second Symphony? Alas, he was not so well informed about it as she supposed, and when he took his leave he was made to feel very distinctly that she was displeased with him.

Occurrences like that perhaps help us to understand why Mahler eventually felt like shouting 'Perish all programmes!'

What Kind of 'Resurrection'?

The question remains, therefore, of how we are to make sense of a work like the Second Symphony – or, to give it the nickname by which it is still widely known, the 'Resurrection' Symphony. Obviously this is not 'music about music'; as with the First Symphony, it is not enough to try to explain it simply in terms of musical argument. The last two movements set texts dealing with matters of faith and doubt, the meaning of life, how belief in a God of Love can be reconciled with the fact of human suffering. It is the second of these poems,

Resurrection Ode by Friedrich Klopstock (1724–1803), that is partly responsible for the symphony's nickname. With the symphony's first movement being a gigantic funeral march, the Second Symphony as a whole can be seen to mark a huge progression from darkness and death through to light and affirmation of life and love.

Mahler took pains in the above-quoted programme (which, incidentally, was written after his 'conversion' to Roman Catholicism in 1897) to make sure that the listener did not identify his concept of 'resurrection' with orthodox Christian doctrine. He said: 'And lo: there is no judgement; there are no sinners; no just men; no great and no small; there is no punishment and no reward! A feeling of overwhelming love imbues us with the bliss of knowing and being.' Those last two sentences are perhaps the most revealing that Mahler ever wrote about his Second Symphony. He may have had his doubts about a benign, omnipotent, personal 'God', but it seems that he never really doubted the transcendent power of love. It is 'knowing and being' that may be the true significance of 'resurrection' for Mahler: a rising from the fear of death or deadness of being into the fullness of life here and now. As in the contemporary play *When We Dead Awaken* by the great Norwegian playwright Henrik Ibsen (1828–1906), the challenge is to rise above mortal fears, to know and be – or, in the words of Klopstock's *Resurrection Ode*, 'Cease from trembling! Prepare yourself to live!' Such sentiments would chime in with those parts of Nietzsche's philosophy which had impressed the young Mahler: a proud atheist and self-proclaimed 'anti-Christian', Nietzsche still believed in the possibility of being spiritually 'born again'.

> Second Symphony as a whole can be seen to mark a huge progression from darkness and death through to light and affirmation of life and love.

From Death to Life: The Narrative of the Second Symphony

Mahler was surely right to drop the original title for the symphony's first movement, *Todtenfeier*. It is not really necessary. After the grimly arresting beginning (low growls from cellos and basses through nervous string tremolos) the music quickly settles into a steady march tempo. The dark orchestral coloring and prevailing C minor mode make it clear that this is a funeral march. Even without Mahler's programme note as a prompt, the anguished tone of some of the writing suggests an element of protest or of fearful questioning: 'What is life and what is death? Will we live on eternally? Is it all an empty dream or do our life and death have a meaning?' A quieter, ardent second theme in the major key (violins) briefly holds out the promise of an answer, but it soon fades back into the funeral march: faster now, and more urgent. The alternation of the two themes, one dark and despairing, the other light and hopeful, continues until the funeral music builds to a granite-like central climax. The certainty of death seems underlined massively at this point. There is a recapitulation, in which the hopeful major-key theme is allowed to expand and intensify, but the funeral tread returns, darker than ever, until the movement is extinguished with a furious final gesture, reminiscent of Macbeth's despairing 'Out, out, brief candle!'

It is 'knowing and being' that may be the true significance of 'resurrection' for Mahler: a rising from the fear of death or deadness of being into the fullness of life here and now.

The next three movements are much shorter. Whether one sees the gentle *Andante moderato* as 'A blissful moment in the life of the dear departed and a sad recollection of his youth and lost innocence' or just a well-placed intermezzo, the music tells us what the programme does not. With its affectionate evocations of the music of Schubert and of the Austrian country dance tunes (especially the waltz-like Ländler) with which Mahler had a lifelong love–hate relationship, it becomes apparent that this movement is 'about' Mahler himself.

After this comes the sinister, sarcastic humour of the third movement, which the programme note (unlike the published score) makes clear is a scherzo. This brings another of Mahler's self-referential musical clues. Much of this music is based on one of the *Knaben Wunderhorn* songs, 'Des Antonius von Padua Fischpredigt' ('St Anthony of Padua's Sermon to the Fishes'), which relates the charming folk legend of how St Anthony, ignored in his preaching by the citizens of a seaside town, turns and preaches to the fish instead. The story, and the reference by the clarinets to Bruckner's Fourth Symphony, ought to suggest simple, childlike faith, but the tone of the music is nervous, even acidic. This would fit well with the programme note's description of how the hero loses 'his perception of childhood and the profound strength that love alone can give' and 'despairs of both himself and God'.

'It can easily happen,' Mahler wrote to Max Marschalk in 1896, 'that this ever-moving, never-resting, never comprehensible bustle of existence becomes horrible to you, like the swaying of dancing figures in a brightly lit ballroom, into which you peer from the dark night outside... from which you perhaps start away with a cry of disgust.' All those elements can be heard in this scherzo. Disgust is more than hinted at in the saccharine trumpet tune of the central section. (Scored differently, it could so easily have been a sweet, inoffensive, folksy tune.) There is no mistaking the terrifying full-orchestral 'cry of disgust' or, according to the programme note, 'despair' near the end of the movement. From this the scherzo dwindles into a sound like a deep bell-stroke (gong, harps, and low horns): a nihilistic death knell.

Blessed contrast follows. The contralto sings the first line of the anonymous folk poem *Urlicht* ('Primeval Light') and winds respond with a simple but dignified hymn tune. Again, this is based on one of Mahler's contemporary *Wunderhorn* songs. An anguished central section reaches its climax at the words 'I am from God and will return to God', then warmth and light return, with a beautiful final sigh on the word 'Leben' ('Life'), a poignant anticipation of the word's crucial appearance in the final movement 'Bereite dich zu leben' ('Prepare yourself to live'). For all its depth of expression, *Urlicht* is very short: in fact it could be seen as a preface to the immense final movement, which begins with a return of the 'cry of disgust/despair' that ended the third movement. So at first it seems as though the simple faith expressed in the *Urlicht* movement has done nothing to banish horror and dread. But gradually a new stillness pervades the music, with distant horn-calls and stirrings of life from woodwind and strings. A woodwind chant recalls the medieval plainsong *Dies irae* ('Day of Wrath'). An anguished cor anglais melody leads to a more sonorous return of the *Dies irae* chant. Then an apocalyptic march section (with offstage bands) builds to an awe-inspiring climax as Mahler paints a quasi-medieval picture of the dead arising for the day of judgement. Mahler must have been thinking here of another composer whose music left a powerful impression on him, the Frenchman Hector Berlioz (1803–1869). Berlioz's monumental Requiem (or 'Grand Mass for the Dead') similarly uses vast forces, theatrically arranged around the church or concert hall, to evoke the terrors and splendour of the Last Judgement.

This huge onslaught culminates in another 'cry of despair', now amplified with fanfares from the enlarged brass section, as Mahler reacts in horror to the orthodox Christian portrayal of 'resurrection'. A moment of stillness, then more offstage fanfares are heard, quietly this time, and enriched with sweet woodwind birdsong – surely the programme note's 'eerie stillness' in which 'we can just barely make out a distant nightingale'. A different view of resurrection is now presented as the chorus enters: 'Rise again, yes, you shall rise again.' Soprano and contralto soloists recall and develop the *Urlicht* music: simple faith now has a role to play. Finally, chorus, full orchestra and organ lead to a thrilling apotheosis on the final lines of the hymn, with their very Mahlerian sentiment: 'What you have struggled for shall carry you to God.' The symphony culminates in massive brass calls and the triumphal chiming of gongs and bells. Amazingly, when this magnificent music is compared with Mahler's 'naïve' programme note, all suggestion of hyperbole in the text vanishes. Mahler does not seem to be overstating the case, as the Second Symphony really can bear that kind of comparison.

It is tempting to read a message of renewed personal hope in the massively affirmative ending of the 'Resurrection' Symphony. Against the odds Mahler had achieved something truly awe-inspiring. It coincided with his discovery of taking a summer break in the Alps, which made composing a real practical possibility. Mahler was now able to make a living from something in which he took artistic pride, his conducting, while simultaneously buying time for his life's real work. Unsurprisingly, the next few years showed a marked increase in his musical productivity.

Against the odds Mahler had achieved something truly awe-inspiring.

Chapter 4

Beyond All Bounds

Beyond All Bounds

The mid-1890s saw Mahler beginning at last to achieve some measure of professional stability. His stay at the Hamburg Opera was the longest in his career thus far, by some margin, and spending the summer in Steinbach established the kind of regular rhythm that was favorable to composition. While he was engaged in conducting, Mahler might jot down ideas or make mental notes for future works, and then entrust them to what the literary critic John Livingston Lowes called 'the laboratory of the unconscious'. Ideas would therefore develop at the back of Mahler's mind while he was consciously occupied with other things, so that by the time he sat down in his composing hut a good deal of important preparatory work and creative gestation had already taken place.

The period was not without its share of stress. The political battles with Bernhard Pollini in Hamburg continued to be a source of strain; then, in February 1895, one of Mahler's two surviving brothers, Otto, shot himself. Otto had also studied music at the Vienna Conservatory, and, following his famous brother, was about to begin a career as an opera conductor. The shock was terrible. Mahler had felt particularly close to Otto, and had often enjoyed discussing music and literature with him. Otto's suicide note contained a phrase that must have affected Mahler deeply: it said that in

killing himself he had 'handed back the ticket' – a quotation *Mahler's composing*
from one of Mahler's favorite novels, Fyodor Dostoyevsky's *hut at Steinbach*
Brothers Karamazov (1880). Ever susceptible to guilt, Mahler
may well have wondered if he had influenced his brother's
decision to commit suicide.

Possessed by Death?

The tragic, premature deaths of Mahler's two favorite brothers
have been put forward as an explanation for the composer's
lifelong preoccupation with death, but the obsession goes
back far further. As a child Mahler had written 'a polka, to
which he had added a funeral march as an introduction.'
How utterly Mahlerian! In Kay Redfield Jamison's classic
study of manic depression and creativity, *Touched with Fire*,
Mahler is placed high on a list of probable manic-depressive
composers. The extreme mood swings in Mahler's music,

directly reflecting his own personality, would be evidence enough for some; but Professor Jamison also points out that manic-depressive tendencies tend to 'cluster' in families: hence Otto's volatility and eventual suicide and Mahler's sister Justi's proneness to terrifying hallucinations of death. Mahler's occasionally almost supernatural productivity (the packed conducting seasons, the furious rate of composition during many of his summer 'holidays') is highly typical of the 'manic' phase of the condition. Manic depressives, Professor Jamison writes, are often preoccupied with death. They also tend to think in spectacularly grandiose terms. In less creative individuals this can lead to dangerous delusions, but when combined with genius, as in Mahler's case, the results can be overwhelmingly impressive. Taken in isolation, Mahler's ambitious programme for his 'Resurrection' Symphony could be read as a symptom of grandiose self-delusion. Yet for most listeners the music really does live up to Mahler's claims for it: proof of Professor Jamison's contention that what we call 'mental illness' can sometimes be a creative blessing, something from which many can benefit.

The Tide Begins to Turn

There was another horrible ordeal for Mahler in 1895. In March he gave the premiere of the first three movements of his Second Symphony in Berlin. There was a pitifully small audience, and the reviews were withering: one critic accused Mahler of 'cynical impudence'. Nonetheless, friends and admirers put up the money for a complete performance in Berlin on 13 December. With memories of the symphony's disastrous part-performance still fresh, this seemed foolhardy; Mahler himself was consumed with anxiety. As

To his utter astonishment, Mahler had scored the first big hit of his compositional career.

the performance progressed he developed a terrible migraine, and at the end he rushed off the stage in a state of near collapse. This time the critics were sharply divided, but the applause was sensational. To his utter astonishment, Mahler had scored the first big hit of his compositional career. The consequences were far-reaching. Among those present was the nineteen-year-old Bruno Walter (1876–1962), later to become one of the twentieth century's greatest conductors. Walter was deeply moved by the experience, and pledged that night to devote himself to Mahler and his music. He kept that promise to the end of his long life.

Mahler must have returned to Steinbach in 1895 with renewed hope. That is certainly the impression given by an important new friend, or rather newly important friend: Natalie Bauer-Lechner, viola player of the Soldat-Roeger Quartet. Natalie had known Mahler from their conservatory days, but in the mid-1890s they grew closer, and she was a frequent guest at the house at Steinbach (Mahler allowed almost no one up to his composing hut). For some time Natalie had been in awe of Mahler and, by 1895, she was almost certainly in love with him too. Alas, her desire was unrequited, but Mahler seems to have valued her intelligent and sympathetic company (perhaps also enjoying her patent adoration), and made no objection to her writing down all she could remember of what Mahler said to her. Eventually she compiled her notes in a book, *Mahleriana*, and it forms the most important record of the composer's thoughts and feelings between 1893 and 1901 – that is, until Alma Mahler took over the role of chronicler. Alma was very dismissive of Natalie in her diaries and *Memories and Letters* – but she was a woman who had no time for rivals.

Mahleriana is fascinating. Natalie clearly knew how to sift the wheat from the chaff. It was to Natalie, for instance, that Mahler described the childhood composition of the polka preceded by a funeral march. Natalie recorded many of Mahler's most revealing anecdotes about his childhood, such as the wonderful story of little Gustav following the military band. Mahler also gave her explanations for some of the mysteries connected with his early years – for example, why so few complete compositions survive from his conservatory days: 'Before even finishing my work, I was no longer satisfied with it. I had already moved beyond it.'

'A Musical Poem': The Third Symphony

Mahler's next symphony, No. 3 in D minor, was the most complex and ambitious piece he had written up till that time. It is a measure of his new confidence and general creative contentment that he finished it in only two summers (1895–6): four years had been spent laboring on the First Symphony, and as many as six were devoted to the 'Resurrection'.

'Everyone knows by now that some triviality always has to occur in my work, but this time it goes beyond all bounds,' Mahler wrote towards the end of the summer of 1896, this time looking forward, with at least a show of gleeful defiance, to the consternation he could expect his Third Symphony to cause the critics. No doubt he was remembering some of the barbed comments in the press after the partial first performance of his Second Symphony the previous year. Far from being chastened, however, Mahler had created a successor to the Second that was even longer and more bizarrely structured. This time there were six movements, the first almost as long as the other five put together. Instead of following (however loosely) the model of Beethoven's 'Choral' Ninth Symphony, as he had in the 'Resurrection' Symphony, this time he mixed elements of symphony, tone poem, Lieder, oratorio and folk music. More bewilderingly, there were extreme juxtapositions of the sublime and the deliberately trivial: the sweetly naïve post-horn melody in the third movement; the children's playground songs of the fifth. Even the First Symphony's parodic funeral march had not taken quite as many stylistic risks. Despite his heroic cheerfulness, Mahler must have braced himself for another massed rejection.

If so, he was in for a big surprise. The premiere of the Third Symphony took place in 1902, in the small German town of Krefeld. It was a triumph, against all the odds. The summer of 1902 was swelteringly hot, the acoustics in the hall were less than adequate, and Mahler, conducting, was forced to work with an ad hoc orchestra, thrown together at the last minute. He was given a standing ovation, and the critics raved. As was so often the case in Mahler's compositional career, however, this turned out to be a false dawn: the symphony's Viennese premiere in 1904 incensed members of the press. One of them, unable to last the whole ninety minutes, left the hall, muttering audibly that Mahler deserved a spell in jail for perpetrating such nonsense. Half a century later, the English composer William Walton summed up the feelings of many of his contemporaries (and not just in Britain) when he remarked, 'It's all very well, but you can't call *that* a symphony'. And yet amid the scandalized, outraged objections there was equally impassioned praise. At that same performance in Vienna, the young composer Arnold Schoenberg (1874–1951), who until then had been rather hostile to Mahler's music, told Mahler ecstatically that the symphony had revealed to him 'a human being, a drama, *truth*, the most ruthless truth!'

It is easy to see why the Third Symphony should provoke such extreme reactions. In both form and content it is Mahler's most outrageous work. The orchestral forces may be slightly smaller than those used in the 'Resurrection'

Symphony or the so-called 'Symphony of a Thousand' (Symphony No. 8); in other respects, however, it is every bit as breathtakingly ambitious, and grandiose dreams again find full artistic justification. Mahler had said that '...the symphony must be like the world. It must embrace everything.' If that all-inclusiveness is the key to his philosophy of the symphony, then the Third may be regarded as his most 'symphonic' work.

Mahler also revealed a great deal about the Third Symphony in letters to the soprano Anna von Mildenburg, one of the stars of the Hamburg Opera, and Mahler's lover at that time:

> Just imagine a work of such magnitude that it actually mirrors the whole world – one is, so to speak, an instrument played upon by the universe... My [third] symphony will be something the like of which the world has never heard! ...In my symphony the whole of nature finds a voice... Some passages in it seem so uncanny to me that I can hardly recognize them as my own work.

Mirroring the whole world also meant giving musical voice to the superb Alpine scenery that surrounded him as he composed the Third Symphony. When Bruno Walter arrived at Steinbach, just as Mahler was completing the symphony, he was momentarily lost in wonder at the magnificence of the mountains. 'You needn't stand staring at that,' Mahler told him. 'I've already composed it all!'

'The Voice of Nature'

There was again the question of how much to tell the audience: would the music speak for itself, or would it need words?

If so, what kind of words? At first Mahler thought about giving the Third Symphony a title. Perhaps, he reflected, it could be called 'Pan', after the Greek god of nature. Another possibility, which Mahler seems to have clung to for rather longer, was 'Die fröhliche Wissenschaft' ('The Joyful Science'), the title of one of Nietzsche's philosophical works. Even though the Nietzsche-based title was eventually dropped, the connection remains in the very fabric of the music. In the symphony's fourth movement Mahler sets the most famous lines from Nietzsche's *Also sprach Zarathustra* ('Thus Spake Zarathustra'). This was the work in which Nietzsche first put forward the idea of the 'Superman', the ideal man who could embrace life (nature) in all its fullness, who could confront both the beauty and the horror of existence not only without flinching, but even with a sense of exultation – in Nietzsche's own words, 'saying "yes" to life'. Up to a point Nietzsche's philosophy found a sympathetic echo in Mahler. After finishing the symphony's second movement Mahler made this very Nietzschean comment:

> It always strikes me as strange that most people, when they speak of 'nature', think only of flowers, little birds and woodsy smells. No one knows the god Dionysus, the great Pan. There now! You have a sort of programme: that is, an example of how I make music. Everywhere and always it is only the voice of nature!

It may be coincidence, or simply an indication of how Nietzsche's ideas were 'in the air' among the German-speaking intelligentsia at this time, but the years 1895–6 also saw the creation of another great orchestral work inspired by Nietzsche: Richard Strauss's symphonic poem (or as he now preferred, 'tone poem') *Also sprach Zarathustra*. It is a very different work from Mahler's Third Symphony, especially in its conclusion – though it is striking that both Strauss and Mahler end by questioning important elements in Nietzsche's philosophy. Having achieved the magnificent climactic vision of the 'Superman', Strauss throws it all into doubt with a strangely ambiguous conclusion, perhaps inspired by the increasing expressions of doubt in Nietzsche's own later works. ('There is no guarantee that the truth, when it is finally uncovered, will even turn out to be interesting,' Nietzsche confides in the darker moments of his *Jenseits von Gut und Böse – Beyond Good and Evil.*) Mahler, on the other hand, would end his Third Symphony by introducing a notion that Nietzsche scorned: divine love, especially as manifest in pity for the lowly and suffering.

Initially Mahler gave the symphony's six movements subtitles: 1. 'Summer marches in'; 2. 'What the flowers of the meadow tell me'; 3. 'What the animals of the forest tell me'; 4. 'What night tells me' (mankind); 5. 'What the morning bells tell me' (the angels); 6. 'What love tells me'. As Mahler later noted, a kind of evolutionary philosophical plan emerges, in which each movement aspires to greater heights than the one before: elements, plants, animals, human beings, angels, God (love). Eventually the titles were dropped and in later performances the Third Symphony appeared without detailed explanatory programme notes. All the same, it is clearer than ever that Mahler does not want us to approach the Third Symphony as 'absolute music'. Even more than in the 'Resurrection' Symphony, there are elements in the Third that cry out for non-musical explanation. How else can we make sense of his choice of texts in the fourth and fifth movements, the incredible diversity of sounds in the first, or the offstage post-horn interjections in the third? There is undoubtedly a message to be read here.

More practically, the newcomer needs to be prepared for the Third Symphony's extraordinary proportions. The first movement is huge: around thirty-five to forty minutes in most performances. Attempts to make sense of its structure along traditional formal lines usually end in sad confusion. At times its fantastic kaleidoscope of wildly contrasting sounds seems to dominate over any idea of a coherent symphonic argument. Once, when out walking with Natalie Bauer-Lechner, Mahler drew attention to a seemingly cacophonous mixture of village sounds: merry-go-rounds, hurdy-gurdies, fairground booths, brass bands. 'Do you hear it?' said Mahler. 'That is polyphony. That's where I got it from.' Nowhere in Mahler's music is that notion of 'polyphony' more apparent than in the first movement of his Third Symphony. Broadly speaking, this movement alternates three kinds of music: the dark, primordial sounds of the opening (described by Mahler as 'Pan awakes'); gentler nature sounds (murmuring wind and string trills, woodwind birdcalls); and raucous, garish fairground and military march music (brass fanfares, dotted rhythms and plenty of glittering percussion). Eventually it is the martial music that triumphs: 'Summer marches in'.

The 'flowers of the meadow' minuet that follows is on a much more intimate scale. It is delicately scored, and full of folksy tunefulness. Mahler was persuaded to let this movement be heard on its own before the whole symphony was performed. It was an instant hit, causing Mahler mixed feelings:

> If I ever want to be heard I can't be too fussy, so this modest little piece will no doubt present me to the public as the 'sensuously' perfumed 'singer of nature'. That this nature hides within itself everything that is frightful, great and also lovely (which is exactly what I wanted to express in the entire work in a sort of evolutionary development) of course, no one ever understands that.

The scherzo third movement is more complex. The naïve vitality of the 'animals of the forest' is twice interrupted by a distant post-horn, sounding through a halo of hushed high strings – a nostalgic memory perhaps, or an evocation of primal innocence. Here Mahler uses a theatrical effect (the offstage post-horn) to suggest distance of another kind: the innocent melody comes to us as though from another time, perhaps a remote, idyllic past. Then, near the end of this movement, comes a ferocious *fortissimo* outburst: Pan is revealed again in all his 'frightful' majesty. Writing about another summer 'holiday' of twelve years later, Alma Mahler recalled a time when Mahler was seriously disturbed by this dark side of nature:

> One day in the summer he came running down from his hut in a perspiration, scarcely able to breathe. At last he came out with it: it was the heat, the stillness, the Pan-ic horror. He was overcome by this feeling of the goat-god's frightful and vivid eye upon him in his solitude, and he had to take refuge in the house among human beings, and go on with his work there.

The great British authority on Mahler, Deryck Cooke, describes this account as 'scarcely credible', but surely Mahler is not alone in feeling sometimes 'spooked' by nature. Listening to the sudden panic-stricken outburst at the end of the Third Symphony's scherzo, Alma's story becomes easier to believe.

Quiet echoes of the deep bass stirrings from near the beginning of the symphony introduce the **fourth movement**, almost all of which is delivered in an awe-struck *pianissimo*. Here the subject is mankind's struggle to make sense of the world, its joy and its grief, as expressed enigmatically in the

Nietzsche verses from *Also sprach Zarathustra*. Then the sound of bells (literally, and mimicked by the boys' choir repeating 'Bimm, bamm') introduces the **fifth movement**. With childlike delight, angels tell of God's forgiveness of Peter, the 'all too human' disciple of Christ who became the rock on which the Christian Church was built.

The sixth movement combines the functions of slow movement and finale, moving from rapt meditation to grand summing-up. An ardent, hymn-like theme for strings (strongly, perhaps deliberately, echoing the slow-movement theme of Beethoven's last string quartet, Op. 135) alternates with troubled, searching music: there is room for doubt here too. Ideas from earlier in the symphony return, then the hymn builds to a grand apotheosis, using the force of the full orchestra (minus the harps) for the first time since the end of the first movement. Mahler confided to Anna von Mildenburg that he had a 'motto' in mind when he wrote this movement:

> *Father, see these wounds of mine! Let no creature of yours be lost! ['Vater, sieh an die Wunden mein! Kein Wesen lass verloren sein!']. I could almost call this* [the finale] *'What God tells me'. And truly, in the sense that God can only be understood as love. And so my work begins as a musical poem embracing all stages of development in a step-wise ascent. It begins with inanimate nature and ascends to the love of God.*

With these words, and the music they summarize, Mahler shows that he has achieved mature separation from Nietzsche's philosophy, while still admiring him. Nietzsche scorned notions of God, pity and redemption; Mahler makes them the stirring culmination of this, perhaps his most 'world-embracing' symphony.

Vienna: Intrigues and Sacrifices

As well as seeing the completion of the Third Symphony, 1896 marked the premieres of *Lieder eines fahrenden Gesellen* and the First Symphony in its revised four-movement form in Berlin. Neither was an unqualified success, but both attracted some praise, publicly and privately. Mahler must have felt that at last he was beginning to 'arrive' as a composer, although for some years to come he remained in the public eye a great conductor first and a composer very much second.

On 11 October 1896 Mahler's conservatory friend and mentor Bruckner died, leaving his Ninth and final symphony very nearly, but not quite, complete. The first performance of the three completed movements did not take place until 1903 (and even then in a bowdlerized version); it left a deep impression on Mahler, which is especially evident in the *Adagio* finale of his own Ninth Symphony.

Mahler was often ambivalent about Bruckner's stature as a composer. He told Natalie Bauer-Lechner that he was 'carried away by the greatness and wealth of Bruckner's invention, but every now and again you are disturbed... by its piecemeal character'. Alma presents a slightly different picture. She recalls, for instance, how, on the title page of his copy of Bruckner's choral *Te Deum*, Mahler crossed out the words 'For solo voices, chorus and orchestra, organ *ad libitum*', and wrote 'For the tongues of angels, heaven-blest, chastened hearts, and souls purified in the fire!' Long after 1896 Mahler continued to conduct Bruckner's music, and to invoke him in his own works as a symbol of an ideal 'simple faith'.

Also in 1896, Richard Strauss became chief conductor at the Munich Opera. Their half-supportive, half-competitive friendship continued, but Mahler does not appear to have been quite so jealous of Strauss's success this time. Perhaps this was because, as a conductor, he had the biggest prize of them all in his sights. Anxious to escape from Hamburg and continued conflict with Pollini, Mahler had carefully kept himself informed about the state of play in Vienna. The Vienna Opera's music director, Wilhelm Jahn, had held the post for seventeen years, and he was now getting old and losing his sight. With Natalie Bauer-Lechner's help Mahler contacted Rosa Papier, a former star mezzo-soprano (she had sung under Mahler in the Kassel performance of Mendelssohn's *St Paul*). Now an influential teacher, she was also having a relationship with Eduard Wlassack, administrative director to the intendant at the Vienna Opera.

Mahler's achievements in Hamburg and Budapest counted very much in his favor. However, his barely concealed affairs with Marion von Weber and Anna von Mildenburg had earned him a reputation as a scandalous womanizer, and there was also Viennese anti-Semitism to contend with. The Emperor Franz Joseph I was no fan of the anti-Semitism factions. He refused to ratify the election in 1895 of Karl Lueger, leader of the virulently anti-Semitic Christian Social Party (and much admired by the young Adolf Hitler). Mahler felt, rightly, that conversion to Roman Catholicism was essential. The Viennese Imperial Court was staunchly Catholic: after all, less than a century before, Vienna had still been the capital of the old 'Holy Roman Empire'. Privately, Mahler made no secret of the fact that this was pre-eminently a political move. He told the critic Ludwig Karpath:

> *The fact is that my longing to escape the hell of Pollini's theatre in Hamburg made me think about withdrawing from the Jewish covenant. That is what is so ignominious about the whole affair. I do not deny that this step, motivated, as*

one might say, by the instinct of self-preservation, cost me considerable effort, even though at heart I was not at all averse to the idea.

This is a very interesting and typically complicated statement. On one level Mahler appears to confirm that his 'conversion' was intellectually insincere, and it is reasonably clear from his later statements that he was never a straightforward upholder of Roman Catholic doctrine. Yet, on another, more emotional level, it does seem that there was something genuine in the move. Since boyhood, Mahler had been attracted by certain aspects of Catholic mysticism, and perhaps also by the strangely moving mixture of high art and kitsch so evident in Austrian church interiors. Alma Mahler confirms this in her *Memories and Letters*, but also indicates the complexity of Mahler's feelings about this apparent renunciation of his Jewishness:

The Jewish question touched Mahler very closely. He had often suffered bitterly from it, particularly when Cosima Wagner, whom he greatly esteemed, tried to bar his appointment in Vienna because he was a Jew. He had had to be baptized before he could aspire to such a high position under the Royal and Imperial exchequer. In any case he had a strong leaning to Catholic mysticism, whereas the Jewish ritual had never meant anything to him. He could never pass a church without going in; he loved the smell of incense and Gregorian chants. But he was not a man who ever deceived himself, and he knew that people would not forget he was a Jew because he was sceptical of the Jewish religion and baptized a Christian. Nor did he wish it forgotten, even though he frequently asked me to warn him when he gesticulated too much, because he hated to see others do so and thought it ill-bred. No one dared tell him funny stories about Jews; they made him seriously angry.

In any case, the pro-Mahler forces in Vienna were becoming more and more vocal. Brahms was dying of cancer, but his earlier praise of Mahler counted for a great deal; and the hugely influential pro-Brahmsian critic Eduard Hanslick was openly on Mahler's side. It began to seem more and more that it was only a matter of time. Eventually Mahler was appointed Hofkapellmeister (Deputy Director) at the Vienna Opera on 8 April 1897, making his debut with a unanimously praised performance of Wagner's *Lohengrin* in May. Then, on 15 October, he was made full director. Mahler's years of greatest glory as a conductor were now about to begin.

As a composer, meanwhile, he was growing still more confident. Creative work was largely ruled out during the summer of 1898, while Mahler recovered from an operation for hemorrhoids in June (a much more dangerous and painful matter in the late nineteenth century than today). It was not until the summer of 1899 that he was able to begin work on the Fourth Symphony. This was to be very different from any of the others so far. At first sight it seems more modest in its aims, as it is in its length and orchestral forces. Yet, in many ways it was to be his most radical and sophisticated work to date.

A Symphonic Humoresque? The Fourth Symphony

In a conversation about the Fourth Symphony, Mahler told Natalie Bauer-Lechner: 'I really wanted to write a symphonic humoresque, but it turned itself into a full symphony, whilst earlier when I wanted it to become a symphony it became the length of three: as with my Second and Third.'

In 1900, just after he had finished the Fourth, Mahler

wrote in more detail to Natalie about how the work had taken shape. He had set out with clear ideas, but then the work had 'turned upside-down' on him:

> To my astonishment it became plain to me that I had entered a totally different realm, just as in a dream one imagines oneself wandering through the flower-scented garden of Elysium and it suddenly changes to a nightmare of finding oneself in a Hades full of terrors. The spoors and emanations of these, to me horrifying, mysterious worlds are often found in my compositions. This time it is a forest with all its mysteries and its horrors which forces my hand and weaves itself into my work. It becomes even clearer to me that one does not compose; one is composed.

Mahler's remarks about 'mysteries and horrors' may surprise readers who know the Fourth Symphony. Writers often portray it as his sunniest and simplest symphony, an affectionate recollection of infant happiness, culminating in a vision of heaven seen through the eyes of a child, with only the occasional pang of adult nostalgia to cloud its radiant blue skies. But Mahler was too sophisticated to fall for the sentimental nineteenth-century idea of childhood as a paradise lost. He knew that children could be cruel (he had not forgotten his experiences at the Prague Gymnasium), and that their capacity for suffering was often seriously underestimated by adults. There is cruelty in the seemingly naïve text Mahler sets in his finale, 'Das himmlische Leben' ('Heavenly Life'), another poem from *Des Knaben Wunderhorn*: 'We lead a patient, guiltless, darling lambkin to death,' the child tells us contentedly, adding that 'Saint Luke is slaying the oxen.' Mahler may have been a carnivore in later years, but during his student days he

had been sufficiently disturbed by man's inhumanity to animals to take up vegetarianism. A moment or two earlier in the Fourth Symphony's song-finale comes mention of 'the butcher Herod', on whose orders the children were massacred in the biblical Christmas story. What are images like these doing in heaven?

Whatever one feels about this ambiguous vision of heaven, Mahler's concluding song movement offers one of the most original and satisfying solutions to the Romantic symphonists' perpetual 'finale problem'. It could not be less like the massive, all-encompassing finales that many composers had struggled to provide in the wake of Beethoven's titanic Fifth and Ninth symphonies, and which Mahler himself had attempted to provide in his first three symphonies.

Interestingly, Mahler composed the Fourth Symphony's last movement before he had written a note of the preceding three, indeed before he had any idea what his Fourth Symphony would be like. At one stage he had thought of including it in his huge Third Symphony (which would have made that mammoth work even longer), but then he began to see it more clearly as the ending of his next symphony. Mahler's ideas continued changing as the new work took shape. At first it was to be a 'symphonic humoresque', but it was then that the ideas took on a life of their own and the symphony 'turned upside-down'. In its final form, the first three movements of the Fourth Symphony prepare the way for the closing vision of 'Das himmlische Leben' on every possible level: not only thematically, but in terms of orchestral colors, tonal scheme (moving from the 'home' G major to E major) and, most of all, its strange emotional ambiguity – blissful dream touched by images of nightmare. Far from being simple, the Fourth Symphony is in fact one of the most subtle things that Mahler created.

Going to Heaven: How the Fourth Symphony Evolves

The very opening of the Fourth Symphony is a foretaste of the finale. Woodwind and jingling sleigh-bells set off at a slow jog-trot, then a languid rising violin phrase turns out to be the beginning of a disarmingly simple tune: Mahler in Mozartian garb, complete with powdered wig. There is a note of contained yearning in the cellos' lovely second theme, but this soon subsides into the most childlike idea so far: a sweetly 'rococo' tune for solo oboe, clarinets, bassoon and horn. Later, another tune is introduced by four flutes in unison: pan-pipes, or perhaps boys cheerily whistling. After this the 'mysteries and horrors' of the forest gradually make their presence felt until, in a superb full orchestral climax, horns, trumpets, bells and glittering high woodwind sound a triumphant medley of themes from earlier on (a glance back at the complex 'polyphony' of the Third Symphony, here distilled into something simpler and more lucid). This triumph is dispelled by a dissonance, underlined by gong and bass drum, before trumpets sound out the grim fanfare rhythm that Mahler was later to use to herald the Funeral March of his Fifth Symphony. How do we get back to the land of lost content glimpsed at the beginning of the movement? Mahler simply stops the music, and the Mozartian theme starts again in mid-phrase, as though nothing had happened. All the main themes now return, but the dark disturbances of the development keep casting shadows, at least until the brief, ebullient coda.

The second movement, a scherzo with two trios, proceeds at a leisurely pace (really fast music is rare in this symphony). Mahler described the first theme as 'Freund Hain spielt auf'; the 'Friend Hain' who 'strikes up' here is a sinister character from German folklore – a Pied Piper-like figure whose fiddle-playing leads those it enchants into the land of 'beyond'. Death in disguise? Mahler evokes Freund Hain's fiddle ingeniously by having the orchestral leader play on a violin tuned a tone higher than normal, which makes the sound both coarser and, literally, more highly strung. Death does not quite have the last word, though the final shrill *forte* (flutes, oboes, clarinets, glockenspiel, triangle and harp) leaves a sulphurous aftertaste.

The slow movement is marked 'Ruhevoll' ('restful'), but the peace is profoundly equivocal. Mahler wrote that this movement was inspired by 'a vision of a tombstone on which was carved an image of the departed, with folded arms, in eternal sleep': an image half consoling, half achingly sad, and clearly related to the Freund Hain/death imagery in the scherzo. The heart-easing, upward string sigh at the start of the movement is in fact a direct quotation from a work that Mahler conducted frequently during his years at the Vienna Opera: Beethoven's *Fidelio*. The same two-chord progression, almost identically scored, opens the famous Act I Quartet from Beethoven's opera. This quotation is surely significant. The first words of the Quartet are sung by poor deluded Marzelline, who believes that she is about to be happily married to the 'man' she loves – except that he is not a man: he is a woman in disguise. Her 'Mir ist so wunderbar' ('It is so wonderful to me') is painfully ironic, and this may connect with the ambiguous 'child's view of heaven' in Mahler's finale. A set of free variations on the first theme explores facets of this ambiguity until Mahler springs a wonderful surprise: a full orchestral outburst of pure joy in E major, the key in which the finale is to end. This passage looks forwards and backwards: horns anticipate the clarinet tune which opens the finale, then recall the whistling boys' flute theme from the first movement. Then the movement slips back into peaceful sleep, to awaken in... paradise (or, at least, a child's version of it).

The sleigh-bells return to open the finale, then the soprano enters for the first time. Possibly fearing what adult singers might get up to if told to imitate a child, Mahler adds a note in the score: 'To be sung in a happy childlike manner: absolutely without parody!' But not, Mahler fails to say, without irony. At the mention of St Peter, the writing becomes hymn-like, preceding those troubling images of slaughter. The singer seems unmoved by what she relates, but plaintive, animal-like cries from oboe and low horn disturb the vision, if only momentarily. At last the music makes its final turn to E major, the key of the heavenly vision near the end of the slow movement. 'No music on earth can be compared to ours,' the child tells us. The child then falls silent and the music gradually fades until nothing is left but the soft, low, repeated tolling of the harp. It is a strange and haunting ending: blissful on one level, disturbing on another. Does Mahler believe in the folk-Catholic vision of heaven that he has just portrayed, or is he wishing that he believed? And there may seem to be just a hint of something 'horrifying' behind this dream of the 'flower-scented garden of Elysium'... That is one of the fascinating things about Mahler: just when he seems to be at his most childlike and simple, he is also at his most adult and knowing.

In this symphony Mahler's neo-Classicism is still a long way from the more clinical, even gleefully sadistic neo-Classicism of Igor Stravinsky (1882–1971). Mahler was not completely detached from the sentimental late nineteenth-century image of Mozart as the 'divine child', a creator of Arcadian Dresden china figurines in music. But in its concentration and lucid musical argument, the Fourth Symphony shows that Mahler's awareness of the meaning of 'classicism' in music went deeper than mere imitation of mannerisms.

Chapter 5

Alma

Alma

By the beginning of 1898 Mahler had installed himself thoroughly at the Vienna Opera, and was setting out the terms of his regime with characteristically ferocious resolve. His relationship with the Imperial Court authorities was, on the whole, far better than it had been with Hamburg's Bernhard Pollini, but he was as irascible and dictatorial as ever, and ruthless in his pursuit of artistic perfection. Inevitably there came complaints from singers and musicians, but generally speaking the critics were warmly appreciative and even some members of the openly anti-Semitic press praised him. His free attitude to tempi and his retouching of the masters were still occasionally criticized, but he defended them no less vigorously than before. Encouraged by the results, the presiding Court officials were inclined to give him plenty of leeway. Natalie Bauer-Lechner records an apparently typical meeting with the Oberhofmeister (Lord Chamberlain), Count Lichtenstein:

Count Lichtenstein summoned Mahler to discuss an argument about a ballet conductor, and tactfully suggested, for he was very impressed with Mahler, that he should avoid fueling the fires of those who complained of his irascibility and impatience. Mahler countered by pointing out that discipline at the Hofoper was appalling, that the level of performance had suffered for many years due to slipshod attitudes and woefully low standards, and that such shake-ups were absolutely necessary. He would only call the house to order if he went to work with the utmost severity. Many people actually agreed with him, he added, and indeed wished for such 'disputes'. In future he would therefore be grateful if the Count were to summon him only at times when there had not been at least two such disputes every week.

One can imagine Bernhard Mahler's approval at this, and perhaps Mahler himself was aware of his debt to the ambitious, brutally determined example of his father. One visitor to Mahler during his Hamburg years remembered him drawing attention to his father's chair, proudly exhibited in the corner of his office.

> Mahler revolutionised the Vienna Opera. At the core of his achievement was his genius as a conductor.

Vienna: The New Regime

The effect of Mahler's appointment was almost immediate. It would be no exaggeration to say that Mahler revolutionized the Vienna Opera. At the core of his achievement was his genius as a conductor. Bruno Walter summed it up thus:

He lived in everything and everything lived in him. And no matter how foreign a sentiment might be to him, how contrary to his character, his imagination would enable him to place himself inside the most opposite person and in the strangest of situations. Thus, Mahler's heart was on the stage when he sat at the desk. He conducted or, rather, he produced the music in accordance with the drama.

This is an amazing display of empathy from a musician often described as 'egocentric'! Mahler's conducting seems to have been as riveting to watch as it was to hear. Extraordinary silhouette images by the Viennese caricaturist Otto Boehler survive and are frequently reproduced. They look like comic exaggerations, but Walter insisted that, in spirit at least, they were entirely accurate: 'Boehler's excellent silhouette caricatures show the violent and drastic nature of his gestures during his first years in Vienna... His agility at that time and also previously, in Hamburg, was astonishing.'

Caricature of Mahler conducting, by Boehler

Mahler's influence at the Vienna Opera extended way beyond the orchestral pit. He hired only the best and most appropriate singers for each part, coached the orchestra and chorus relentlessly, and took full responsibility for the stage direction and costumes, all of which were in a pretty miserable state at the time Mahler arrived at his post. One of his far-reaching decisions was to bring in a brilliant designer, Alfred Roller (1864–1935), in 1903. Roller made an instant impact with his designs for Mozart's operas (which Mahler championed at a time when few other opera houses took Mozart seriously), and also for Wagner's music dramas and Beethoven's *Fidelio*. One of Roller's most talked-about innovations was his use of two towers on the set for Mozart's *Don Giovanni*. These remained on the stage throughout the opera, changing their function as scenery according to the needs of each scene. Today such ideas are commonplace in opera productions, but in Mahler's day it was a breakthrough, and much appreciated by audiences and critics.

Also in 1898 the Vienna Philharmonic Orchestra voted in Mahler as its own musical director, indicating that, at least at this stage in his career, Mahler's artistic results were valued more than his tactics were feared. The following year, Mahler bought a plot of land at the Alpine village of Maiernigg, overlooking the lake, the Wörthersee. He built his 'Villa Mahler' on this land, and in 1900 erected his new composing hut above the house in the woods nearby. It was here that he completed his Fourth Symphony and began the Fifth. His summer regimen, however, was still as strict and demanding as in the opera house. His sister Justi and devoted chronicler Natalie Bauer-Lechner were guests in the house, but during the day they saw little of him as he buried himself in composition in his woodland cell.

Love at First Sight?

In November 1901 came the decisive meeting with the woman Mahler was to marry: Alma Schindler (1879–1964). The word 'decisive' is used carefully here because although Alma tells us, in *Memories and Letters*, that this was her first meeting with Mahler (at the house of her friend Bertha Zuckerkandl) it turns out that she had already met him during her holidays in the summer of 1899. This is not the only time Alma rewrites, or perhaps one should say 'creatively adjusts', history.

Alma was a remarkable woman. She came from a highly artistic family, her father being the painter Emil Schindler (1842–1892). He was a leading exponent of what came to be called 'atmospheric impressionism' – perhaps best described as the Austrian equivalent of the French impressionism of Camille Corot (1796–1875). Alma adored her father, but he died when she was just entering her teens, after which her mother promptly married one of his students, Carl Moll. Alma strongly resented her mother's decision, and she inveighed against Moll repeatedly in her diaries.

> In November 1901 came the decisive meeting with the woman Mahler was to marry: Alma Schindler a highly gifted, imaginative, passionate and intelligent woman.

Alma was also a composer of some talent. She studied with the Austrian-Jewish composer Alexander Zemlinsky (1871–1942), with whom she was soon having an intense, not quite consummated relationship (her diaries are breathtakingly frank on this subject). The affair with Zemlinsky was still going on at the time she met Mahler, and seems to have continued for a while afterwards. Alma's diaries reveal her mental torment as she tries to choose between the two men, both of whom powerfully attracted her. They also confirm the impression left by *Memories and Letters* that she was a highly gifted, imaginative, passionate and intelligent woman, and

Alma Mahler, pictured c. 1910

there are occasional hints of a ruthlessness that came close to matching that of her future husband.

Memories and Letters has come in for some criticism in recent years. It is true that Alma embellished the story of her relationship with Mahler, in the process creating myths that some scholars have been at pains to correct. Nevertheless, *Memories and Letters* is gripping, fascinating and very readable. As the Viennese-born critic and musicologist Hans Keller put it: 'There isn't a boring line in this racily written book'. Some of her descriptions of and insights into Mahler's working life are hard to disbelieve; but if she was occasionally guilty of myth-making, hers were nevertheless very good myths – stories that helped many listeners find their way into Mahler's complex scores at a time when there was still widespread resistance to his music.

Her feelings for, and even estimation of, Mahler were highly complicated. Initially, like so many of her contemporaries, she was much more impressed by him as a conductor than as a composer. Her diaries show that she made sustained efforts to like his music, and yet one wonders whether she succeeded in this. Early in their relationship she scandalized some of Mahler's friends by stating bluntly that she did not care much for her future husband's music, and her attitude seems to have remained ambiguous for most of her long life. Clearly she enjoyed her status as Mahler's widow in her later years, when his star as a composer was in the ascendant. One cannot help noticing that from the list of composers whose music she chose to have played at her funeral, his name was absent.

As for Mahler's attitude to Alma, he adored her. The terrible suffering of his last years, which he poured out not only in letters but in the manuscript of his last symphony, the Tenth, shows how much he dreaded losing her. It is also clear that he patronized this girl, nearly half his own age.

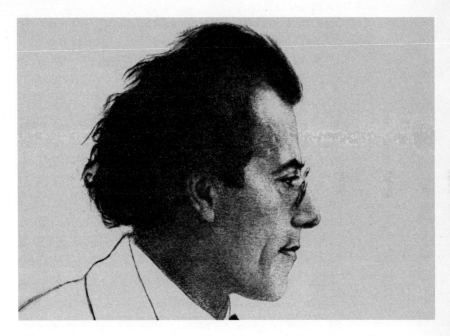

There were ominous signs almost from the very beginning. *Mahler by*
Take this extraordinary demand, made in a letter that Mahler *Emil Orlik, 1902*
wrote to Alma from Dresden on 19 December 1901, three
months before they were married. One thing, he insists, has
to be set straight immediately:

> *From now on, would you be able to regard my music as
> if it were your own?... A husband and wife who are both
> composers: how do you envisage that? Such a strange
> relationship between rivals: do you have any idea how
> ridiculous it would appear, can you imagine the loss of self-
> respect it would later cause us both... One thing is certain: if
> we are to be happy together, you will have to be 'as I need you',
> not my colleague, but my wife!*

It makes uncomfortable reading. Mahler thinks that he
is taking an enlightened, modern view of marriage, not a

'philistine view', yet here he is telling her effectively to kill the thing that she loves, to deny herself the possibility of artistic 'children'. Reading these words, it is hard not to feel for Alma. She made a determined effort to fall in with his command, but it is evident how much the effort cost her.

There was clearly something about Mahler that made Alma prepared to contemplate such extreme self-sacrifice, and she seems to have sensed this almost immediately. In her account of their first proper meeting, Alma says that she mostly ignored him, forming a cool appraisal of his strengths and faults in company. But her private diary presents a different kind of impression: 'I must say, I liked him immensely, though he's dreadfully restless. He stormed about the room like a savage. The fellow is made entirely of oxygen. When you come close to him, you get burnt.'

It was to be the beginning of a dramatically intense, vitally important and often very difficult relationship. The courtship was brief; then, despite the misgivings Alma must have had about her husband's demands, they married on 9 March 1902. Whatever its effect on Alma, for Mahler marriage sparked an extraordinarily new creative period. It is hard to resist the impression that Mahler was a man who needed to love and, once he had decided to do so, loved volcanically. Inevitably for an artist whose raw material was his personality and experience, the effect on his music was profound.

Songs of Love: *The Rückert Lieder*

The first signs of this effect can be seen in the group of songs that Mahler composed in 1901–2. These are usually grouped together as *Fünf Lieder nach Rückert* (*Five Rückert Songs*), although this was not Mahler's title, and the songs do not form an organic song cycle like *Lieder eines fahrenden Gesellen* or the later *Kindertotenlieder*. At least two of them can be seen as containing messages for Alma, and one has important connections with his next symphony, the Fifth.

The German poet Friedrich Rückert (1788–1866) tends nowadays to be dismissed, or at least damned with faint praise, by critics: in the *Oxford Companion to German Literature* he is described as 'fertile and facile... his large output of poetry is more notable for its neat workmanship in various verse forms than for vision and originality'. Mahler very rarely set German poetry of the very first rank, yet he was undoubtedly a man of sophisticated literary taste. So what was it about Rückert's verses that drew the attention of a composer with 'vision and originality' in abundance? Mahler knew that Rückert was not a great writer, but this, he revealed, was part of the attraction. Setting a sublime poem to music was, he said, a form of sacrilege, 'as if a sculptor chiselled a statue from marble and a painter came along and colored it'. But Mahler was not simply looking for bland material to which he could add his own musical coloring. As with the folk poetry of *Des Knaben Wunderhorn*, Rückert's rhythms lend themselves naturally to musical setting; more importantly, Rückert's poetry was full of the kind of subject matter that would have appealed strongly to Mahler. This was to become clearer still in *Kindertotenlieder*, also based on Rückert, which Mahler began at about the same time as his *Rückert Lieder*.

The Rückert songs do not have a common theme, nor did Mahler indicate a definite order in which they should be performed; but they fit together very effectively. The unifying theme is Mahler himself: his loves, his thoughts on life, his playful sense of humour. With the exception of the more

> Mahler knew that Rückert was not a great writer, but this, he revealed, was part of the attraction.

heavily scored 'Um Mitternacht', they are marvels of delicate, chamber-music-like orchestration. 'Liebst du um Schönheit' was not actually orchestrated by Mahler, but by the musician and critic Max Puttmann, who in 1916 made a convincing job of imitating the master.

'Ich atmet' einen linden Duft' ('I breathe a delicate scent') is the most chamber-like of all the five songs in its forces: just five woodwind instruments, two horns, harp, celeste and no string basses. Mahler could not find a direct musical equivalent for Rückert's punning on 'Linde' ('lime tree') and 'linde' ('gentle'), so he paralleled it in fabulously delicate touches of orchestration such as the opening ripples of sound for harp, celeste, clarinet and viola harmonics. 'Blicke mir nicht in die Lieder' ('Don't look for me in my songs') – its scoring like air-blown thistledown – is an affectionate warning to the curious, with only the lightest touches of irony: the artist will reveal all in good time. Did Mahler write this with Alma in mind? There is no mistaking the message of 'Liebst du um Schönheit' ('Do you love for beauty's sake?'), however, and Mahler made sure that Alma got it. He slipped the manuscript inside a copy of Wagner's *Die Walküre* which Alma had been reading through at the piano, and waited for it to fall out 'magically' when she opened the pages. Unfortunately it did not, and the exasperated Mahler had to pick up the score himself, supposedly on a whim, so that the song could fall out in front of her. 'I was overwhelmed with joy', Alma recalled, 'and we played it that day twenty times at least'. It is curious that this was the only one of the Rückert songs that he never orchestrated.

There is an element of longed-for escape in the exquisite **'Ich bin der Welt abhanden gekommen'** ('I am lost to the world'), which is for most critics the pearl of this set. For much of the year, with his work at the Vienna Opera, Mahler

CD 2
track 1

www.naxosbooks.com

was only too deeply entangled in the 'world's commotion' (Rückert's expressive German word is 'Weltgetümmel'). The idea of abandoning oneself to love, music and 'peace in a still land' says a great deal about what those precious summer holidays meant to him. If the string writing at the phrase 'in meinem Lieben' ('in my love') sounds familiar, that is because Mahler quotes it in the closing bars of the famous *Adagietto* fourth movement of the Fifth Symphony: a reference that he evidently hoped Alma would hear and understand.

In 'Um Mitternacht' ('At midnight'), however, the subject is not peaceful resignation, but steely resolution. Mahler clearly felt that this harder message demanded harder sounds, so the strings, usually at the core of Mahler's most personal expression, are silent. Instead, the heavy brass (trumpets, trombones and tuba), double bassoon and timpani appear for the first and only time. There is also a plaintive new instrumental color, the oboe d'amore – midway between oboe and cor anglais and still rarely used in the modern symphony orchestra. At the end, the full ensemble, with swirling harps and piano, intone an unmistakably religious cadence: a resounding 'Amen' as the poet yields his destiny to God.

Mahler at Maiernigg: An Intimate Portrait

Echoes of that apparent religious resolution can also be heard in the Fifth Symphony, especially in its closing pages. Mahler wrote this symphony, the first to appear in public without either programme or sung text, in 1901–2. It was the first major work to be fully written in the new composing hut at Maiernigg. In *Memories and Letters* Alma describes in detail Mahler's routine there. This little portrait, although not without affection, gives some idea about how difficult it must have been to be around Mahler during these summer 'holidays':

> *Mahler's daily programme during the next six summers at Maiernigg never varied. He got up at six or half past and rang for the cook to prepare his breakfast instantly and take it up to the steep and slippery slope to his hut, which was in a wood nearly two hundred feet higher up than the villa. The cook was not allowed to take the usual path, because he could not bear the sight of her, or indeed of anyone whatever, before setting to work; and so, to the peril of the crockery, she had to scramble up by a slippery, steeper one. His breakfast consisted of coffee (freshly roasted and ground), bread and butter and a different jam every day. She put the milk on a spirit-stove, matches beside it, and then beat a hasty retreat by the way she had come in case she might meet Mahler climbing up. He was not long about it; he was very quick in all he did. First he lit his spirit-stove, and nearly always burnt his fingers, not so much from clumsiness as from a dreamy absence of mind. Then he settled down comfortably at the table and bench in front of the hut. It was simply a large stone building with three windows and a door. I was always afraid it was unhealthy for him, because it was surrounded by trees and had no damp-course; but he was so fond of this retreat that I could do nothing about it.*

Even when he was not at his desk in the hut, Mahler's mind would not stop working. Sometimes he and Alma would take afternoon walks together, but these too might well be interrupted by the muse:

> *Often and often he stood still, the sun beat down on his bare head, he took out a small notebook, ruled for music, and*

wrote and reflected and wrote again, sometimes beating time in the air. This lasted very often for an hour or longer, while I sat on the grass or a tree-trunk without venturing to look at him. If this inspiration pleased him he smiled back at me. He knew that nothing in the world was a greater joy to me. Then we went on or else turned for home if, as often happened, he was eager to get back to his studio with all speed.

Alma's statement that 'he knew that nothing in the world was a greater joy to me' has an ironic undertone. Mahler may have been serenely convinced that his artistic self-absorption was a source of joy to his wife, but was Alma? Only two lines later she draws attention to his 'remarkable egocentricity', and expressions of frustration, open or half-concealed, litter these pages. However, she paints a very memorable picture of life at Maiernigg, and often the minute details are as telling as her more general observations. She notes, for instance, that at the time he was writing the Fifth Symphony, Mahler kept copies of Bach's music in his composing hut. He had apparently been stung by allegations that his music lacked real counterpoint: the kind of musical texture in which one hears several equally contending 'voices' rather than simple tune-plus-accompaniment. So his choice of the greatest of all contrapuntal masters to keep him company as he wrote the Fifth Symphony has to be significant. Mahler developed a vigorous personal contrapuntal style of his own in the Fifth Symphony: the finale's complex fugal writing is an exhibition of his new-found mastery.

Dangerous Disparity? The Fifth Symphony

There is naturally much more to the Fifth Symphony than technical display. As with all his works, the symphony bears the imprint of Mahler's life experiences at the time. It was begun in the summer before his 'decisive' meeting with Alma. But even with a composer like Mahler, one should be careful about reading life-events too literally into the music. The sudden change of mood between the second and third movements, from tragedy to wild elation, surely cannot indicate that Mahler met Alma between finishing one movement and beginning the next. Yet it is striking how many writers have felt that, in emotional character, the Fifth Symphony is 'dangerously disparate' (to use Deryck Cooke's much-quoted phrase). It begins in sepulchral darkness, with Mahler's most impressive funeral march thus far, and ends in a mood of wild affirmation. The scherzo's astral fireworks after the bleak ending of the second movement do indeed come as a surprise. But here, as much as in his previous symphonies, Mahler has a story to tell; even if there is no programme to help us make sense of it, plenty of clues are given along the way.

> Most critics now agree that Mahler was probably the supreme master of the 'narrative symphony.'

Most critics now agree that Mahler was probably the supreme master of the 'narrative symphony': the kind of symphony which, whatever its purely musical strengths, also seems to tell a non-musical story. Commentators may argue about what the story in question might be, but few dispute that it exists, in some form or other. Mahler would have agreed, even if he himself couldn't give the exact details. He was careful to stress that his works were not simple autobiographies in sound, and while biographical details may shed light here or there, they are never the final 'explanation.' As Mahler suggests, if we are to find the true message, we must be prepared to ponder a little harder than that.

Some of the symphony's moods and dramatic happenings can be explained by relating them to events in Mahler's life at the time. The year in which he began the symphony, 1901, had been a turbulent period. In February, after a near-fatal hemorrhage, Mahler had resigned as conductor of the Vienna Philharmonic Orchestra. Under his dictatorial regime, the initially co-operative orchestra had grown restive – often with at least an undercurrent of anti-Semitism. Such strife and a close encounter with death may well have left their marks on the opening Funeral March and on the turbulent *Allegro* that follows. 'Messages' for Alma are associated with later stages of the work, particularly the famous **Adagietto** (in the form of the quotation from 'Ich bin der Welt abhanden gekommen' from the *Rückert Lieder*).

As to the wider meaning of the symphony, there are several clear signposts in the music. The opening of the first movement is terrifying: a trumpet fanfare in C sharp minor, quiet at first but growing menacingly. At its height, the full orchestra thunders in with a funereal rhythm; then, to an accompaniment of shuddering string trills, horns bring this huge paragraph to a close, ending on a deep, rasping G sharp. The imagery seems clear: death in full grotesque pomp. But then comes a change in perspective in the first trio section. The quieter march theme in the strings is clearly related to the song 'Der Tambourg'sell' ('The Drummer Boy'), another setting from *Des Knaben Wunderhorn*, which Mahler also composed in 1901 when beginning the Fifth Symphony. The song tells of a pitiful soldier boy facing execution for desertion. Both the March's trio sections bring a degree of contrast, but the atmosphere remains dark and oppressive. Not even the desperate full-orchestral outburst just before the end, marked 'Klagend' ('Lamenting'), brings release. So the first movement confronts us with death as seen from different angles: grand collective mourning in the opening fanfares, and a more

> The imagery seems clear: death in full grotesque pomp.

private, wretched grief in the song-inspired first trio section. The end is almost brutally curt; there are ghostly reminders of the opening fanfare on muted trumpet and flute, a distant bass drum roll, then a violent pizzicato from lower strings.

In the stormy second movement, Mahler develops and intensifies the mood of the Funeral March's first trio. Broadly speaking, this movement is an urgent, sometimes painful struggle. The three-note woodwind figure heard after the initial low, growling string figures soon comes to embody the idea of striving: its three notes strain upwards, then fall with a little sigh. (Mahler foreshadowed this figure at the violently lamenting climax of the first movement.) Several times, aspiration falls back into desolate contemplation, sometimes with flashbacks to the Funeral March; but gradually a new note of hope is increasingly heard. At last the striving culminates in a radiant brass chorale, with ecstatic interjections from the rest of the orchestra. There is a strong resemblance here to the old German carol 'Wie schön leuchtet der Morgenstern' ('How brightly shines the morning star'). Is the answer to death to be found in religious consolation, something like Bruckner's 'simple faith'? And yet the glory here is illusory, unstable, and the movement quickly fades into minor-key darkness, life this time extinguished by quiet string-bass pizzicatos and a solitary drum tap.

A surprise follows. The **scherzo** bursts onto the scene with a wildly elated horn fanfare. The character is unmistakably Viennese, a kind of frenetic waltz. Perhaps some of Mahler's mixed feelings about his adopted Viennese home went into this movement. But this appears to have little to do with the struggles between death and hope in the first two movements. At this point some commentators have labelled the Fifth Symphony 'schizophrenic', but, if Professor Kay Redfield Jamison's ideas hold good, 'manic-depressive' would be more appropriate. Many of Mahler's friends and colleagues observed in his behavior the extreme mood-swings typical of the condition. Some psychologists have suggested that the over-elated manic phase represents a deliberate (but partly unconscious) attempt by the mind to escape in flight from unbearable thoughts or situations. Certainly there are parts of this movement where the gaiety sounds forced, even downright crazy. Mahler himself wondered what on earth people would think of it, as he recorded in a remarkable letter to Alma from Cologne on 14 October 1904, while he was preparing for the symphony's premiere:

> *Everything went tolerably well. That scherzo is an accursed movement! It will have a long tale of woe! For the next fifty years conductors will take it too fast and make nonsense of it. And audiences – heavens! – how should they react to this chaos, which is constantly giving birth to new worlds and promptly destroying them again? What should they make of these primeval noises, this rushing, roaring, raging sea, these dancing stars, these ebbing, shimmering, gleaming waves?... Would that I could perform my symphonies for the first time fifty years after my death!*

The images of 'rushing, roaring sea' and 'dancing stars' are wonderful: once read, never forgotten. The scherzo is, on the whole, very different in mood from the previous two movements, but the musical substance is another matter; few of the symphony's critics seem to have noticed this. The thematic 'skeleton' of the scherzo's opening horn fanfare is the same three-note striving and sighing figure that opened the second movement and was foreshadowed in the first. The scherzo may be 'constantly giving birth to new worlds', but these grow from the musical seed planted in the Funeral March and developed in the second movement.

Still, the challenge remains of reconciling the extremes of mood represented by Part One (the Funeral March and the second movement) and Part Two (the scherzo). Perhaps the famous *Adagietto* that begins Part Three can provide a clue. It seems clear now that Mahler intended this movement as a kind of instrumental declaration of love: a 'song without words' to Alma. In the *Adagietto* he uses only the strings, the warmest and most expressive section of the orchestra, plus the liquid tones of the harp. And at the end comes the reference to 'Ich bin der Welt abhanden gekommen' ('I am lost to the world') from the *Rückert Lieder*. The song ends with 'I live alone in my heaven, in my love, in my song', and it is the violin phrase accompanying 'in my love, in my song' that Mahler quotes at the very end of this *Adagietto* movement. It is an incredibly tender moment, but just how private is it meant to be? Mahler must have realized that, one day, lovers of his music would recognize the quotation and read his message to Alma for themselves.

> It seems clear now that Mahler intended this movement as a kind of instrumental declaration of love: a 'song without words' to Alma.

Significantly, it is this invocation of human love and song which provides the real turning-point in the Fifth Symphony. The finale is a vigorous, joyous contrapuntal display: a more robust, earthy kind of joy this time, not the scherzo's manic elation. It begins with another reference to one of Mahler's songs: the *Knaben Wunderhorn* setting of 'Lob des hohen Verstandes' ('In praise of lofty intellect'), which tells of a song contest between a nightingale and a cuckoo, judged by a donkey. The donkey chooses the cuckoo, because his song is easier to understand and, in fact, is rather like his own melodious cry! It is quite possible that this is Mahler's answer to his critics, especially those who had accused him of a lack of contrapuntal skill. Certainly the finale's counterpoint grows more muscular and intricate from this simple, humorous beginning; even motifs from the *Adagietto* are drawn into the textures. Finally, after a long and exciting build-up, the second movement's brass chorale returns in full splendor, now firmly anchored in D major, the symphony's ultimate home key. Is this the triumph of faith, hope and love? Not everyone finds the ending convincing. Alma herself had major reservations, and some listeners may find themselves in agreement with her:

> *In the autumn he played me the completed Fifth Symphony. It was the first time he had ever played a new work to me and we climbed arm in arm up to his hut with all solemnity for the occasion. When he had done, I told him of all that won my instant love with this magnificent work, but also that I was not sure about the chorale at the end. I said it was hymnal and boring. He disagreed.*
>
> *'Yes, but Bruckner,' he protested.*
>
> *'He, yes; but not you,' I said, and on the way down through the wood I tried to make clear to him the radical difference between his nature and Bruckner's. I could not feel he was at his best working up a church chorale.*
>
> *I was touching here on a rift in his being which often went so deep as to bring him into serious conflict with himself. He was attracted by Catholic mysticism... His love of [it] was, however, entirely his own.*

It is possible to hear the ending of the Fifth Symphony either as joyous affirmation or as strained triumphalism, half-concealing a lingering trace of doubt and dread. In either case, it can still be deeply moving. Even if one feels that Mahler fails, wholly or partly, to reach the summit that he strives for, the failure itself can be full of pathos. It is also possible that Mahler is expressing not so much faith in the Christian notion of divine love as faith in its human equivalent: the redeeming love that he believed himself to have found in Alma. By the time he came to write his Eighth Symphony (dedicated to Alma), Mahler was keen to assert that there was no real difference between divine love and human 'creative' love. Could Alma then be the true 'morning star' of the old German carol invoked at the symphony's conclusion? If so, it is more than a little ironic that she found it 'hymnal and boring' – possibly indicative of troubles to come.

However the Fifth Symphony is taken as an expression of Mahler's personal hopes and fears, there is a universal message to be read here. Searching within himself, Mahler again finds something that can speak to and for each one of us. For all his apparent late-Romanticism, Mahler – in being philosophically ahead of his time – can also be seen as a very modern composer: even in his most seemingly positive statements there is often a shadow of doubt. If, in the inner recesses of his heart, he realized that the simple faith symbolized by the chorale was no longer possible, he was giving expression to a feeling which, in the century to come, increasing numbers of people would begin to share.

Chapter 6

Heights and Depths

Heights and Depths

On 3 November 1902, just eight months after the Mahlers were married, Alma gave birth to their first child, Maria. It was a breech birth: in other words, the baby emerged backside first. For Alma the labor was not only acutely painful but also highly dangerous. For Mahler too the whole experience was a hellish ordeal, but once Maria was born and presented to him there followed one of those spectacular mood-swings which so often seem to match his music (as in, for example, the Fifth Symphony). One minute all Mahler can focus on is suffering and the possibility of death; the next he is wildly elated by life and cracking jokes. Alma tells the story in *Memories and Letters*:

> *Owing, as the doctor said, to the fatigues I had undergone during my pregnancy, the child had got misplaced. Mahler was not told of this, for fear of agitating him; but he read it in the faces of the doctor, the nurse and my mother, and raced through the streets as though frantic. When a friend of his, Guido Adler, asked how I was, he shouted at him: 'Idiot, I forbid you to ask me.' I could hear him raging up and down in the next room, waiting in a frenzy of anxiety for the end of this frightful delivery. When at last it was over, he cried out: 'How can people take the responsibility of such suffering and*

keep on begetting children!' He was crying hard when he came
to my bedside. When I told him subsequently that it had been
a breech birth he laughed uncontrollably. 'That's my child.
Showing the world straight off the part it deserves.' He loved
this child beyond measure from the first day.

Mahler named her Maria, in honour of his mother, though she
soon acquired the nickname 'Putzi' (an old-fashioned German
expression for 'pretty'). Alma was right: Mahler adored his
daughter from the very first. They became extremely close,
and he even allowed her later to join him in his composing
hut. The above account does not, however, reveal all that
was going on in Alma's mind, and her private diary reveals
something that she, understandably, did not admit to in her
published *Memories:* 'To bring her into the world cost me
incredible pain. I don't yet feel real love for her.'

Tensions at Home

Alma's main preoccupation, though, was her struggle to
accept the role that Mahler had allotted her: the wife of an
artist rather than a creative talent in her own right. While still
pregnant she wrote in her diary: 'my mission, to remove every
obstacle from the path of this genius, is profoundly fulfilling.'
Yet only a few weeks after Putzi's birth there is this painful
entry: 'I feel as though my wings have been clipped. Gustav,
why did you bind to you this splendid bird so happy in flight
when a heavy grey one would have suited you better?'

Is she here thinking of Natalie Bauer-Lechner, Mahler's
previous devoted chronicler? The 'heavy grey bird' description
is very much in keeping with her previous comments about
Natalie. Now, having won the prize, Alma seriously doubted
whether it was worth fighting for – whether the cost to herself

of marrying this extraordinary man had been exactly as she had anticipated on their first meeting: 'when you come close to him, you get burnt.'

The strains increased after the birth of the Mahlers' second child on 15 June 1904. This was another daughter, baptised Anna, who soon became known as 'Gucki' because of her wide, staring eyes (the German verb *gucken* means 'to peep' or 'to stare'). During the Alpine summer vacations Alma found herself increasingly bored, being expected to take the role of ancillary or child-minder while Mahler immersed himself in his hut. At the same time she was acutely jealous of the admiring women who flocked around Mahler at the Vienna Opera. His minutest flirtations are recorded in her diaries, all in contemptuous terms. After one such incident she exclaims: 'My God! If only he never came home again. Not to live with him any more! I'm so agitated I can scarcely write.' Things got worse when Mahler's lover from his Hamburg days, Anna von Mildenburg, resurfaced at the Vienna Opera. There was at least one showdown. Mahler realised that Alma had turned cold on him and, during one of their walks, he claimed straight out that she did not love him. Alma could not disagree, but in the same diary entry she tells us that 'suddenly my feelings were all there again. Once more I know how much I love him. I am determined to be calm.' When it came to mood-swings, Gustav and Alma Mahler were well matched.

Slightly more alarming are Alma's wide fluctuations of feeling for children. One moment she is full of her love for them, proud of Maria's looks and her closeness to her father; the next we find flashes of almost murderous hatred. In a diary entry for the summer of 1904 she sarcastically refers to them as her 'dear little brats'; but then the word 'brats' is carefully deleted and the more innocuous 'children' substituted.

Triumphs in the Theatre

Meanwhile in Vienna Mahler was sending out shock waves as an opera conductor and director. In 1903 he collaborated with Alfred Roller on a work that always had special significance for him: Wagner's *Tristan und Isolde*. The central themes of love and death, of desire and longing experienced with an intensity close to sickness, the erotic-mystical significance accorded to night – all of this was emotional home territory for Mahler. (He must have had Tristan's eulogies to night at the back of his mind when he called the second and fourth movements of his Seventh Symphony 'Nachtmusik' – 'Night Music.') Alma says in *Memories and Letters* that her own involvement with the visual arts (partly the legacy of her beloved painter-father) was an influence on Mahler, and this must have been the case. Apart from the evocation of Callot's *The Huntsman's Funeral* in the First Symphony, Mahler never referred to paintings when commenting on his earlier works. Now, with Alma's help, he was able to take a proprietorial interest in Roller's designs, breathing new life into the process of opera production. Some of the conservative press hated Mahler's innovations, but there were even louder cries of acclaim. Few seem to have doubted the historical significance of Mahler's achievement.

Some of the conservative press hated Mahler's innovations, but there were even louder cries of acclaim. Few seem to have doubted the historical significance of Mahler's achievement.

In 1904, Mahler and Roller turned their attention to another opera of huge importance for Mahler: Beethoven's *Fidelio* – the opera from which Mahler had directly quoted at the opening of his Fourth Symphony's slow movement. As with *Tristan*, there is so much in *Fidelio* that was guaranteed to appeal to Mahler – in particular the moving depiction of how an idealistic prisoner, held in darkness, is rescued by a brave and determined woman. Despite the strains in his relationship with Alma, Mahler still seems to have clung to the idea that she was in some way his 'rescuer', his 'redeemer'. The Eighth Symphony, which Mahler dedicated to Alma, closes with a final exultant hymn to the 'eternal feminine' who similarly redeems the soul of the 'striving' Faust.

Mahler's 'Tragic' Symphony: The Sixth Symphony

The summers of 1903 and 1904 were enormously productive in terms of composition. It was at this time that Mahler sketched and completed one of his most ambitious and, for many modern commentators, most important works: his Sixth Symphony. When Mahler began work on the Sixth in 1903, he thought about giving it a title: 'Tragic'. Given that Mahler's work often mirrors his life, this may seem strange. He was at the height of his powers as conductor and composer, and in both fields he was enjoying ever greater success with audiences and critics. When the Sixth Symphony was first performed, in 1906, the title was absent; it was there for the Viennese premiere in 1907, but was then permanently dropped soon afterwards.

'Tragic' remains most commentators' verdict on the emotional content of this work, however much the shading of that interpretation may vary. For the conductor Bruno Walter, the Sixth was 'bleakly pessimistic... the work ends in hopelessness and the dark night of the soul'. Mahler's biographer Michael Kennedy identifies something more positive in the symphony's message: 'It is a tragic work, but it is tragedy on a high plane, classical in conception and execution.'

For Mahler there was clearly a dark mood at the heart of the Sixth Symphony, especially in the huge finale. In *Memories and Letters*, Alma is quite specific:

The first page of Mahler's autographed score of his Sixth Symphony

...[the Sixth Symphony is] the most completely personal of his works, and a prophetic one also... In the last movement he described himself and his downfall or, as he later said, of his hero: 'It is the hero, on whom fall three blows of fate, the last of which fells him as a tree is felled.' Those were his words.

Before long these words were to acquire an added eerie significance – a significance that Alma was keen to stress, in the process creating an aura of almost supernatural mystery around the symphony. In 1907, she points out, the year after the symphony's far from successful premiere, 'three blows of fate' did indeed fall on Mahler. First his four-year-old daughter Maria, his adored 'Putzi', died of scarlet fever; then he was diagnosed as having a potentially fatal lesion of the heart; finally, in August, various intrigues and anti-Semitic campaigning forced Mahler to resign his post at the Vienna Opera.

There are good reasons to be doubtful about some of this. Certainly the death of Putzi was shattering for Mahler, as was his heart diagnosis, but his resignation from the Opera was by no means the straightforward 'blow of fate' that Alma claims (especially not one that 'felled him as a tree is felled'). If there was a third fatal blow, it came later, near the very end of Mahler's life.

To the myth-makers, however, all this was a gift. Deep in his prophetic soul Mahler had sensed his own fate and spelled it out in music. Some went even further: Mahler had not just foretold his own grim future, he had looked into the abyss of the coming century and foreshadowed its horrors with devastating power. Where else could those violent march rhythms, those vivid depictions of vanquished hopes and crushed innocence, have come from? It has to be conceded, however, that the myth probably did the symphony more good than harm. Mahler may have been reluctant to provide it with a programme, but Alma's account surely helped a great many new listeners find their way through the intellectual and emotional labyrinth of this long and complex work.

There is another reason why Mahler, at the height of his Viennese career and revelling in his new domestic happiness, might have wanted to write a 'Tragic' Symphony. The idea of tragedy was central to Nietzsche's world view, especially in early works like his culturally ground-breaking *Die Geburt der Tragödie* (*The Birth of Tragedy*), which Mahler also knew. Nietzsche here put forward the idea that the 'classical' tragedies of the Ancient Greeks represented some of the sanest – or, as he put it, 'healthiest' – achievements of mankind, created 'out of the most profound need'. In tragic art, the Greeks had been able to look 'with bold eyes into the dreadful destructive turmoil of so-called world history as well as into the cruelty of nature', and thereby create an art that was 'uniquely capable of the tenderest and deepest suffering'. One can imagine how words like those must have struck straight at Mahler's heart. Nietzsche argued that by confronting the horror of the world through the medium of tragedy, the spectator could acquire the courage to face the horror and meaningless cruelty of existence.

Certainly Mahler's attitude to Nietzsche fluctuated in later life. In 1901, he told Alma, on finding that her library contained a complete set of Nietzsche's writings, that the books 'should be cast then and there into the fire'. But according to the conductor Otto Klemperer, who worked with Mahler from 1905, the composer remained 'an adherent of Nietzsche' to the end. In either case, it is unlikely that when Mahler called his Sixth Symphony 'Tragic' he had forgotten the view of tragedy expressed in a book that had made such an impact on him.

Nietzsche's ideas would without a doubt have appealed to an artist obsessed with death, suffering and the apparently arbitrary cruelty of life, and who strove continually to make sense of it all. Perhaps Mahler's 'Tragic' Symphony can be seen as a sustained attempt to do just that in music: to express Nietzsche's 'yes to life' in the face of all that he felt life could throw at him.

If so, that might account for a paradoxical aspect of the Sixth Symphony. However violent, pained or ultimately bleak the emotions it expresses, there is also something exciting, exhilarating, even uplifting about much of it. It is as though Mahler were at the same time exulting in his mastery, his ability to express what Nietzsche called 'the artistic conquest of the terrible' with such power and virtuosity. After all, the Sixth is one of those works in which Mahler's command of the orchestra is at its most dazzling. In his handling of the huge forces, including instruments never before used in a symphony (celeste, cowbells, whip, and a hammer to represent the blows of fate), not to mention one of the largest woodwind and brass sections in the standard repertory, Mahler reveals himself as a brilliant orchestral magician as well as a tragic poet.

As Michael Kennedy points out, the Sixth is the most 'Classical' of Mahler's symphonies in formal layout. For the first and only time in his symphonic cycle, Mahler's original design follows something like the archetypal four-movement plan developed by Haydn, Mozart and Beethoven. There is a sonata-form first movement (even including an old-fashioned first-section repeat), a slow movement and scherzo, followed by a formally much more complex but still superbly proportioned finale. Moreover, unlike many of Mahler's symphonies, the Sixth follows standard procedure by beginning and ending in the same key: A minor. In Nietzsche's idea of the 'classical',

> For the first and only time in his symphonic cycle, Mahler's original design follows something like the archetypal four-movement plan developed by Haydn, Mozart and Beethoven.

sanity was expressed by the containment of intense, even volcanic emotions in lucid, well-balanced structures. In his Sixth Symphony Mahler seems determined to show that he can do the same: expressing his feelings with the utmost force while fully 'mastering' them in something like traditional symphonic form.

Detailed analysis of such a complex, ninety-minute symphony, packed with incident from start to finish, would fill a sizeable book; a few pointers are nevertheless helpful. In the first movement, two main themes – an intense march tune and an impassioned major-key melody – are juxtaposed, developed at length, then brought back in something like their original form, leading to a triumphant conclusion in the major key. The movement also introduces another of the symphony's most important recurring ideas, the so-called 'fate' motif: a bright major chord followed by a dark minor chord, underlined by martial rhythms on percussion. Alma tells us that the impassioned major-key second theme was intended by Mahler as a portrait of her: 'Whether I've succeeded, I don't know; but you'll have to put up with it,' she quotes him as saying. This raises questions: why, for instance, does the theme on first appearance transform itself into a strutting military march, with glittering glockenspiel? It is the reappearance of this alleged 'Alma' theme that clinches the first movement's final major-key triumph. At the heart of the movement, however, in the midst of all the violence and passion, is a passage of magical stillness, with atmospheric contributions from celeste and offstage cowbells: in Mahler's words 'the last terrestrial sounds penetrating into the remote solitude of mountain peaks'. Here, even more than in the Third Symphony, Mahler has distilled something of the spirit of peace and mystery that he found amid Alpine scenery. Adding cowbells could so easily have been crudely pictorial;

119

instead it is a magical touch, particularly when performed in a hall with a reasonably spacious acoustic.

Mahler was unsure about the order of the middle two movements of the Sixth Symphony. Originally the **scherzo** followed the first movement, but after the symphony was published Mahler changed his mind, and placed the *Andante moderato* slow movement second. There is still a good deal of controversy about this: some commentators feel that the effect of the scherzo immediately 'crushing' the first movement's triumph is too good to miss; others think that if the *Andante moderato* comes after the scherzo its message of peace and consolation is diminished, and that the scherzo's grimly fragmented ending makes a better preparation for the finale. Many conductors still prefer the original order.

Placed after the intense drama of the first movement, the *Andante moderato* is like a haven of peace: meditative, songful, an exploration of the Alpine solitude glimpsed in the first movement. The cowbells, offstage in the first movement, are now played within the orchestra: a telling change in perspective. But there is bitterness and intense, even desperate, longing mixed in with the sweetness.

Relentless, pounding march figures begin the scherzo, the return to the minor mode now negating both the fragile peace of the *Andante moderato* and the major-key triumph of the first movement's ending. This time, however, the violence has a grotesque, sardonic edge. Even the seemingly innocent trio theme (introduced on the oboe) has a strange, limping four-plus-three rhythm. According to Alma, this is one of the Sixth Symphony's most disturbingly prophetic moments: 'In the third movement he represented the arhythmic games of the two little children, tottering in zigzags over the sand. Ominously, the childish voices became more and more tragic, and at the end died out in a whimper.' Perhaps Mahler did have in mind some kind of depiction of innocence corrupted and destroyed at this point, as at several other places in his symphonies and songs. But Alma's attempt to connect it with her own children is weirdly forced: after all, only one of them died, and why then would Mahler mark this passage 'Altväterisch' ('old-fashioned' or 'fusty')? Without Alma's 'programme', it might seem that Mahler was instead mocking the neo-Classicism of his own Fourth Symphony: the work inspired by both the sweet joys and the horrors of childhood. The ending of the scherzo is hollow and desolate, with fragments of the trio's motifs on double basses, contrabassoon and timpani. It has to be said that Mahler does appear to take a grim satisfaction in the destruction of his 'childish voices'.

The finale is like a vast summing-up of all that has been heard before, fused into a complicated but astonishingly compelling musical narrative. In a good performance it can be hard to believe that the movement actually lasts more than half an hour. By turns weird, desolate, heroically determined, joyous and catastrophically thwarted, this music hardly ever seems to relax its precipitous forward progress.

The first two of Mahler's 'three blows of fate' are underlined by the hammer, each time shattering the preceding mood of growing optimism. Then, for some reason, Mahler removed the third hammer blow. It originally fell just before the bleak coda, coinciding with the final appearance of the major–minor 'fate' motif which is this time delivered with the full force of Mahler's much-expanded orchestra. Whether he deleted it for superstitious or more practical reasons is hard to tell. Even today, some conductors shrink from restoring the third blow, apparently afraid of tempting fate. In any case, the most

> The finale is like a vast summing-up of all that has been heard before, fused into a complicated but astonishingly compelling musical narrative.

121

devastating stroke is left to the end. Tuba, trombones and low horns develop a grim threnody, then a full orchestral chord of A minor falls like an iron curtain, leaving the march rhythms to tail off into nothing. This ending is strikingly anticipated at the conclusion of Mahler's youthful cantata *Das klagende Lied*, but the idea had obviously been maturing at the back of his mind and its effect here is far more devastating.

Mahler and Strauss: Friends or Rivals?

Whatever Mahler's philosophical ideas behind the Sixth Symphony's rejected title 'Tragic', he did regard the work as one of his most 'personal' achievements, and its failure to impress at its premiere in 1906 in the German town of Essen was a blow in itself. According to Alma, the whole experience also emphasized the spiritual gulf between Mahler and his friend Richard Strauss. She describes the rehearsals thus:

> *None of his works moved him so deeply at its first hearing as this. We came to the last rehearsals, to the dress rehearsal, to the last movement with its three great blows of fate. When it was over, Mahler walked up and down in the artists' room, sobbing, wringing his hands, unable to control himself... Suddenly Strauss came noisily in, noticing nothing, 'Mahler, I say, you've got to conduct some funeral overture or other tomorrow before the Sixth. Their mayor has died on them. So vulgar, that sort of thing. But what's the matter? What's up with you? But...' and out he went as noisily as he had come in, quite unmoved, leaving us petrified.*

Was Strauss's blustering insensitivity quite as symptomatic of his attitude to Mahler's music as Mahler suggests? To underline her point Alma quotes a remark made by Strauss after the first performance:

I was planted ceremoniously next to Strauss at supper. 'Why ever does Mahler smother his effect in the last movement?' he said. 'He gets his fortissimo *and then damps it down. Can't understand that at all.' He never did understand. He spoke simply as the showman.*

Alma is as barbed as ever, especially when it came to Mahler's older friends. She may have had a point. But, as she concedes earlier, 'Mahler was so afraid that his agitation might get the better of him that out of shame and anxiety he did not conduct the symphony well,' in which case Strauss's incomprehension is easier to understand.

Strauss's reaction does seem to bear out a much-quoted comment by Mahler about his artistic relationship to Strauss: 'I see the whole of him, whereas he sees only my pedestal.' Yet Strauss's championship of Mahler's music, at a time when he had few supporters as a composer, should not be under-estimated. At the Krefeld premiere of the Third Symphony in 1902 it was Strauss who walked to the front of the hall at the end of the first movement to lead the applause (clapping between the movements of a symphony was still acceptable in Mahler's day). On another occasion the ever-changeable Mahler compared himself and Strauss to two men tunnelling into a mountain from opposite sides: 'Eventually we will meet in the middle,' he concluded. Alma scathingly reports Strauss's frequent remarks about the commercial aspects of his work, which she interpreted as a particularly crass form of boasting: at heart, she says, Strauss was little more than a 'travelling salesman'. According to Alma, Mahler was completely in agreement, but if so that may well have been a mark of his jealousy at Strauss's huge international success. Mahler also

> Mahler compared himself and Strauss to two men tunnelling into a mountain from opposite sides: 'Eventually we will meet in the middle,' he concluded.

took offence at the way Strauss divided his attention among people in public instead of concentrating on his 'most important friend' – others might well have seen Strauss's behavior as simple good manners. Alma records an occasion when Strauss invited Mahler to lunch in the company of the conductor Leo Blech. On returning to Alma, Mahler fulminated:

> *And as he (Richard) divides the sunlight of his favor so absent-mindedly and conventionally between me and Blech, the friendly and respectful concern I show for him on such occasions is scattered to the winds, without an echo and probably without even being noticed. I am totally at a loss with myself and the world when this happens to me over and over again! Are people made of different stuff than I?*

Years after Mahler's death, when Alma's *Memories and Letters* was published, Strauss underlined that final question in his own copy of the book, and in answer scrawled an emphatic 'Yes'.

'Tempting Fate'? Kindertotenlieder

The score of the Sixth Symphony was finished in 1904 (though Mahler continued to revise the orchestration, almost until the end of his life). The same year also saw the completion of a second set of songs to poems by Friedrich Rückert – a genuine song cycle this time, and one of the greatest in the repertoire. The five texts Mahler set in this song cycle, *Kindertotenlieder* ('Songs on the Deaths of Children'), touched on the issue that haunted Mahler, and which apparently found its most disturbing expression in the scherzo of the Sixth Symphony: the fragility of young, innocent lives. It was the loss of two children within the space of a week that had prompted Rückert to write the poems. One of those children was called Ernst, like the favorite brother Mahler had lost in his teens. Mahler was enormously susceptible to that kind of 'fateful' coincidence. When he showed the score of *Kindertotenlieder* to Alma, on completing it in the summer of 1904, she was horrified:

> *I found this incomprehensible. I can understand setting such frightful words to music if one had no children, or had lost those one had. Moreover Friedrich Rückert did not write these harrowing elegies solely out of his imagination: they were dictated by the cruelest loss of his whole life. What I cannot understand is bewailing the deaths of children, who were in the best of health and spirits, hardly an hour after having kissed and fondled them. I exclaimed at the time: 'For heaven's sake, don't tempt providence!'*

Mahler had begun these songs in the summer of 1901, however, long before having children of his own had been a realistic prospect. In fact, he had probably finished three of the five songs before that meeting with Alma in November 1901. Alma would have us believe that the grieving mother described so poignantly in song No. 3 ('Wenn dein Mütterlein') is, in some eerily prophetic way, herself; but it could easily be Mahler's memory of his own mother's grief at the death of Ernst. Death, and particularly the death of young innocents, haunted Mahler throughout his life, and this might be another symptom of his probably depressive temperament. Perhaps he was consciously attempting to exorcise a painful memory in writing this cycle, in which case that, rather than some dreadful prophetic intuition, might explain the disturbing musical imagery in the scherzo of the Sixth Symphony. As long as *Kindertotenlieder*, and the act of exorcism it represented, remained incomplete, the ghost would continue to haunt Mahler's creative imagination. Or could it simply be that this was another example of that imaginative power 'to place himself inside the most opposite person and in the strangest of situations' noted by Bruno Walter in Mahler's opera conducting? It is also possible that Alma's reaction, recorded above, was partly influenced by guilt: her diaries reveal that there had been more than one occasion when she had consciously wished her children dead.

However one views its artistic purpose, conscious or unconscious, *Kindertotenlieder* is a superb cycle. It is perfectly possible to perform any of the earlier Rückert songs in isolation; but to take any of the *Kindertotenlieder* out of context would be close to irreverence. Beautiful as they are individually, in context they mean so much more. The sequence begins with a cold depiction of sunrise following the night in which the children died: 'Nun will die Sonn' so hell aufgeh'n' ('The sun will rise just as brightly as before'). Mahler takes a risk in scoring the opening so barely: just oboe and horn, then bassoon, supporting the voice's lamenting phrases. The expression is quietly agonized, and yet one also notices the chamber-like delicacy (this time truly prophetic of musical things to come) and the elegant counterpoint. Mahler's study of Bach in an effort to improve his contrapuntal skills coincided with his beginning *Kindertotenlieder* in 1901. The results are as telling here, in their far simpler way, as at any point in the contemporary Fifth Symphony. There is even an echo of the poignant solo oboe writing in Bach's *St Matthew Passion*. The sparing use of the warm stringed instruments heightens the effect of desolation.

In No. 2, 'Nun seh' ich wohl, warum so dunkle Flammen' ('Now I see why such dark flames'), the eyes of the dead children shine down on their father. The longing cello phrases at the beginning are moving enough in themselves, but since the previous song uses the strings with such restraint, the effect is more powerful. The cellos' phrases are soon connected by the singer with the words 'O Augen!' ('Oh eyes!'), which means that whenever that motif returns, the image returns with it. Then comes No. 3, 'Wenn dein Mütterlein' ('When dear mother'). The mother carrying a candle into the father's study reminds both parents of the little light they have lost. There are more sparse, neo-Bachian textures, then comes the moment of supreme sadness, 'O du, o du, des Vaters Zelle...' ('Oh you, oh you, a part of your father...'): the candle can only light the father's room for a little while. Mahler marks this line 'Mit ausbrechenden Schmerz' ('With an outbreak of pain'), but the note is hardly necessary. No singer would miss the emotional message contained in this aching, soaring phrase.

No. 4, **'Oft denk' ich, sie sind nur ausgegangen!'** brings warmer colors and harmonies. The ideas will be familiar to anyone who has experienced grief: 'Often I think they've only gone out, they'll soon be back.' In the final line Mahler surpasses himself in the expression of simultaneous deluded joy and agonizing loss: the children have just gone for a walk in the mountains: 'Wir holen sie ein auf jenen Höh'n im Sonnenschein! Der Tag ist schön auf jenen Höh'n!' ('We'll find them again on the heights in sunshine! The day is beautiful on those heights'). The singer's line would be quoted with terrible poignancy by the violins in the final dying moments of the Ninth Symphony, thereby negating the criticism that the end of the Ninth is all egocentric leave-taking.

So far the tempo has been prevailingly slow, the orchestral writing sparing. The final song, **'In diesem Wetter, in diesem Braus'** ('In this weather, in this tempest'), is a strong contrast. Rushing string trills and lashing pizzicatos suggest driving rain – a pitiless storm. The parent distractedly thinks of protecting children from the rain and wind: 'What was

I thinking, letting them out in weather like this?' But then the storm blows itself out; a strange light flashes (piccolo, glockenspiel, harp, and high cello harmonics), and the mood becomes warm, tranquil and unforgettably tender: 'Sie ruhn, als wie in der Mutter Haus' ('They rest, as though they were in their mother's house'). The grave becomes a place of comfort and safety. The storms of life can no longer harm the children. Gently lapping string figures are joined by the celeste, Mahler's innovatory addition to the orchestra in the Sixth Symphony; but where its high tinkling sounds enhanced the ethereal stillness of the 'Alpine' passages in the symphony, here it is the instrument's lowest notes that are put to telling use, like the tolling of soft bells. There are reminders of the deep notes at the end of the Fourth Symphony, with its concluding 'child's view of heaven'. It is possible to see the end of *Kindertotenlieder* as a more 'grown-up' answer to the Fourth Symphony's concluding vision: sadder, darker, but still offering hope of peace, whether or not that peace is to be found, in the singer's words, 'in God's protecting hand'.

Chapter 7

A Hymn to Eros

A Hymn to Eros

During the years 1905–6 Mahler was still going from success to success at the Vienna Opera. The revival of his and Alfred Roller's production of Mozart's *Don Giovanni* (with the innovatory 'twin pillars') on 21 December 1905 was, if anything, an even greater triumph than its first performance. It should be borne in mind that the status Mozart enjoys today as, in effect, the official 'world's greatest composer' is largely a twentieth-century phenomenon. In the nineteenth century, even in Mozart's own adopted city of Vienna, his operas were still widely considered rather lightweight next to Beethoven's *Fidelio* and Wagner's great music dramas. Mahler is therefore a crucial figure in the modern Mozart revival: one of the many ways in which he left an indelible mark on the musical attitudes of our time.

While Mahler's reputation as a composer may have lagged some way behind his still-growing fame as a conductor, it now began to catch up. Publishers were starting to show interest in his music, and even to compete for it. The Fifth Symphony, *Kindertotenlieder* and the five *Rückert Lieder* were all published in 1905. There were more performances of his works too (and not only under his own direction), though critical reception still tended to be mixed at best. However, Mahler found an important champion in the

Mahler in the loggia of the Vienna Opera House, 1907

Dutch conductor Willem Mengelberg (1871–1951), for many years director of the Amsterdam Concertgebouw Orchestra. Thanks to Mengelberg, Amsterdam became an enduring 'second home' for Mahler's music, establishing a tradition of Mahler performance (broken only by the years of the Nazi occupation) that continues up to the present day.

'Song of the Night': The Seventh Symphony

The two summers of 1905 and 1906 were a period of incredible productivity at Mahler's summer retreat in Maiernigg. First came the completion of the Seventh Symphony in 1905. Mahler had started the work in 1904, the same summer in which he completed the Sixth Symphony and *Kindertotenlieder*. It requires some effort to conceive how a single mind could have poured out so much complex and fantastically imaginative music in the space of those few summer holidays, even a mind as awe-inspiringly active as that of Gustav Mahler. Initially the Seventh Symphony caused Mahler a major creative headache. First of all he composed two movements, each unlike anything he had ever written before. He gave them both the title 'Nachtmusik' ('Night Music'), a description of their general mood and atmosphere, but also an indication that their role in the larger context of a symphony was to be far from conventional. The problem was that Mahler at this stage could not see what kind of larger symphonic entity might provide a suitable frame for them. When he returned to Maiernigg in 1906 he still seems to have been unsure about it. Knowing of his initial perplexity, some commentators have inferred that he had set himself an insoluble problem, one he never satisfactorily resolved. This seems to have been borne out by the symphony's fate in the concert hall and, more recently, in the record catalogues. For decades

Mahler's Seventh was his 'problem' symphony, but from the start it always had its passionate supporters. When Arnold Schoenberg heard the symphony in 1909 (the year after the first performance) he wrote enthusiastically of its 'perfect repose based on perfect harmony'; but few others have used phrases like 'perfect repose' to describe the Seventh Symphony, and even some of Mahler's most fervent admirers have found the structure far from harmonious. The middle three movements, it is claimed, seem to belong to a world of their own (nocturnal, fantastic, sometimes sinister), a world to which the outer movements, impressive as they are, emphatically do not belong.

> For decades Mahler's Seventh was his 'problem' symphony, but from the start it always had its passionate supporters.

There are other ways in which the Seventh Symphony appears strangely divided. The first two movements glance backwards to the 'Tragic' Sixth Symphony. The energetic leading theme of the *Allegro con fuoco* first movement (after a long slow introduction) recalls the ominous march tune which opens the Sixth; the cowbells and 'fateful' major–minor chord progression in the first 'Nachtmusik' also strongly echo Symphony No. 6. The finale on the other hand often seems to be straining towards the confident expression of mass feeling in the first movement of the Eighth Symphony, the 'Symphony of a Thousand'. According to some critics, the problem of the Seventh Symphony is at least partly explained by a letter that Mahler wrote to Alma in 1910, in which he tells her how the work eventually came into being:

> *In the summer before* [1905], *I had planned to finish the Seventh, of which the two* Andante *['Nachtmusik'] movements were already completed. Two weeks long I tortured myself to distraction, as you'll well remember, until I ran away to the Dolomites! There the same struggle, until finally I gave up*

and went home convinced that the summer had been wasted.
At Krumpendorf... I climbed into the boat to be rowed across
the lake. At the first stroke of the oars I found the theme (or
rather the rhythm and the character) of the introduction to
the first movement... and in four weeks the first, third and fifth
movements were absolutely complete!

However, the story that a work of art tells in itself is often very different from the story of how it was written. Many of the finest works in the symphonic repertoire have had difficult births. Sibelius's magnificent Fifth Symphony took nearly seven years, and two radical revisions, to arrive at its familiar form, and yet the music is so organic that it is hard to believe that it was not conceived in a single flash of inspiration. Also, the song-finale of Mahler's Fourth Symphony was originally intended as an extra movement for Symphony No. 3, and yet it was made to form a completely logical, satisfying finale to the Fourth.

Mahler's Seventh Symphony may be enigmatic and far from self-explanatory; but performed with conviction it can also be uniquely fascinating – unsettling sometimes but far more compelling than many a more conventionally 'perfect' symphony. In no other work of Mahler is the orchestral imagination so highly charged. It isn't simply that the scoring includes instruments rarely seen in the symphony orchestra: tenor horn (a relative of the euphonium), mandolin, guitar, cowbells and deep-pitched bells. Even the familiar instruments are made to produce surprising new colors: the clarinet shrieks and cello and bass 'snap' pizzicatos (the strings plucked so hard that they spring back and smack against the fingerboard) in the scherzo; the dense chorus of woodwind trills

> Mahler's Seventh Symphony may be enigmatic and far from self-explanatory; but performed with conviction it can also be uniquely fascinating.

near the start of the first 'Nachtmusik'; the deep harp tones in the second; the headlong timpani flourishes that set the finale in motion. The orchestral writing is as brilliant as it is challenging to play. If any of Mahler's symphonies deserves to be described as a 'concerto for orchestra', it is the Seventh.

Mahler tells us that the deep, dragging rhythms that open the first movement were inspired by the oar strokes as he crossed the lake to his summer home at Maiernigg. Without knowing this, the listener might well conclude that here is another *echt*-Mahlerian funeral march. Perhaps the oar rhythms fused in Mahler's imagination with the image of Charon, the ferryman of Hades, carrying the souls of the dead to their last resting-place (as in Rachmaninov's almost contemporary tone poem *The Isle of the Dead*). Above this are heard the bellowing tones of the tenor horn; according to Mahler this is a 'voice of nature', but if so it is nature in one of its more ambiguous aspects, sinister as well as impressive. This hugely expanded slow introduction leads to an equally expanded main *Allegro* with a strenuous, striving first theme eventually yielding to a slower impassioned violin melody that strongly recalls the 'Alma' theme from Symphony No. 6. At the movement's heart is a magnificent visionary slow section, in which magical nature imagery is married to a radiantly transfigured version of the 'Alma' theme. Then, suddenly, the radiance is clouded by a return of the opening funereal rhythm, with the sinister 'voice of nature' now on tenor horn and a disillusioned-sounding solo trombone. What, one may ask, is 'nature' trying to say here?

After the first movement's almost frenzied major-key ending, the opening of the first **'Nachtmusik'** comes as a wonderful contrast. Mysterious quiet horn calls (echoed by another horn, muted) are followed by some of Mahler's most fabulous woodwind writing. In all his symphonies

CD 1
track 6
www.naxosbooks.com

Mahler treats his woodwind section with an imaginative freedom unmatched by any of his contemporaries, but this is spectacular even by his standards. One by one the woodwinds enter with trills, turns and arabesques, until at the height of the crescendo there are twelve fully independent woodwind parts in play. Meanwhile, underneath this teeming texture, the opening horn call is sounded repeatedly by the tuba. The effect is like a bizarre dawn chorus except, of course, that this is night, not dawn. At its height, trumpets, horns, timpani and bass drum recall the 'fate' motif from the Sixth Symphony, which is curiously in keeping with the notion of a 'false dawn'. From this emerges a slow nocturnal tread, as in the earlier *Lieder eines fahrenden Gesellen* recalling Schubert's outcast Wanderer.

Mahler also claimed that this movement was inspired by Rembrandt's famous painting *The Night Watch*, another deeply atmospheric, ultimately ambiguous study in shades of darkness. The cowbells from the Sixth Symphony now enter, accompanying the return of the opening mysterious horn calls. Whereas the meanings of Mahler's sound-symbols were relatively clear in the Sixth Symphony, here they remain tantalizingly inscrutable. The ending is especially enigmatic: the clamour of the woodwind chorus now dissolves (again via the 'fate' chords) into quiet gong and cymbal strokes, a deep horn note, and finally a high whispered harmonic on cellos.

The scherzo that follows is marked 'Schattenhaft' ('shadowy'): the nocturnal theme continues. This movement is often described as a 'dance of death' and, although Mahler never described it as such, the tag is hard to refute. Like the central scherzo of the Fifth Symphony, this movement is full of wild, fantastical transformations of Viennese popular music (especially the waltz), but the barbed and acerbic orchestral colors, and the weird, almost hallucinogenic treatment of the leading ideas, suggest that Mahler is now taking a more embittered view of his adopted city's musical culture. This is nowhere more apparent than at the very end, where the waltz's typical oom-pah-pah accompaniment is briefly but violently dissected by timpani and pizzicato violas.

Similar sarcasm might have been expected from the conventionally romantic string cadence that opens the second 'Nachtmusik' (and which Elgar might have featured in one of his popular salon pieces). What follows, however, is much subtler than that. This music is luscious, velvety, exquisitely delicate, with hushed suggestions of an underlying erotic charge. The use of mandolin, guitar and harps underlines the serenade-like character, yet here, just as in the scherzo, there are deep shadows, suggestions of something sinister, never quite explicit. The ending is magically ambiguous. (What a symphony of enigmatic endings this is.) A quietly chuckling low trill twists at last into a sweetly decorous little turn: a wry smile to end one of Mahler's most fascinating symphonic miniatures, at once innocent and knowing.

A tremendous fanfare, led by a breathtaking virtuoso fusillade on timpani, heralds the rondo finale. After all the strange nocturnal goings-on in the symphony so far, this blaze of C major light seems to announce unequivocally that the night has passed, and the day's activity now begins with force. This is the point at which many of the more sympathetic critics finally fall out with Mahler's Seventh Symphony. To call the movement a failure as music is to slander some brilliant invention, but it is very long and much of the activity seems like rather pointless bustling about. Even Deryck Cooke felt that 'Mahler had written for once the thing he most detested: *Kapellmeistermusik*'. Worse, it is difficult to understand how this movement can be seen as in any way a 'goal' or 'summing-up' of the symphony's progress so far.

Mahler rehearsing his Seventh Symphony with the Czech Philharmonic Orchestra in 1908

There is something faintly desperate about the return of the first movement *Allegro* theme near the end, enhanced though it is with chiming 'triumphant' bells. The Fifth Symphony's ambiguous final triumph had been strategically prepared earlier in the work, but only a truly determined conductor can bring off the ending of the Seventh convincingly. Defenders of the symphony sometimes justify this ending as an another example of Mahlerian irony, but even if one accepts that Mahler means something other than what he appears to be saying, the length and rather static activity of the finale as a whole is difficult to take. Mahler was one of music's greatest ironists (perhaps the greatest of all), but his genius for double meanings is done no service if it is invoked to justify rare failures like this finale. Perhaps the best approach to the Seventh is to see it as four-fifths of a great symphony, and enjoy its triumphs for what they are.

This is, after all, more than most critics were prepared to concede when Mahler's Fifth, Sixth and Seventh symphonies were first performed. Today, doubts about the endings of Nos 5 and 7, when they are expressed at all, are usually qualified by admiration for his extraordinary achievements in the earlier stages of those works. The attacks in Mahler's own day, though, undermined his confidence and forced him into nervous, even feverish revisions, particularly of these three great purely orchestral symphonies. After Mahler's death, Schoenberg pointed an accusing finger at those he considered to be stupidly uncomprehending critics:

> How will they seek to answer for this: that Mahler had to say: 'It seems I have been in error'? How will they seek to justify themselves when they are accused of having brought one of the greatest composers of all time to the point where he was deprived of the soul, the highest recompense for a creative mind, the recompense found when the artist's faith in himself allows him to say: 'I have not been in error'?

'The Eternal Feminine': The Eighth Symphony

Mahler's arrival at his Alpine summer retreat in 1906 brought with it yet more creative anguish, but soon afterwards he experienced perhaps the most prodigious musical outpouring of his entire career: the Eighth Symphony, nicknamed the 'Symphony of a Thousand' for the immense forces it employs, which he is said to have composed in an amazing eight weeks. It would take a good eight weeks simply to copy this vast score, let alone compose it! According to Alma, Mahler was initially unable to see what kind of symphony he wanted to compose, as with the Seventh Symphony. This time he found the answer in response to a kind of mental prayer for inspiration:

After we arrived at Maiernigg, there was the usual fortnight during which, nearly every year, he was haunted by the specter of failing inspiration. Then one morning just as he crossed the threshold of his studio up in the wood, it came to him: 'Veni creator Spiritus'. He composed and wrote down the whole opening chorus to the half-forgotten words. But music and words did not fit it: the music had overlapped the text. In a fever of excitement he telegraphed to Vienna and had the whole of the ancient Latin hymn telegraphed back. The complete text fitted the music exactly. Intuitively he had composed the music for the full strophes.

For the text of the second part of the symphony, Mahler was struck by a singularly bold idea.

Veni creator Spiritus is the title of a medieval Catholic hymn, reputed to have been composed by the ninth-century Archbishop of Mainz, Rabanus Maurus: 'Come, Holy Ghost, our hearts and minds inspire'. Alma's account of how Mahler got the rhythms of the setting 'intuitively' right, even when his conscious memory failed him, may sound fanciful; but many creative people report similar experiences. Certainly the setting of the hymn in Part One of the Eighth Symphony is very felicitous: Mahler clearly relished the sounds as much as the rhythms of the Latin words, as Stravinsky was to do, to very different effect, in his choral *Symphony of Psalms* (1930).

For the text of the second part of the symphony, Mahler was struck by a singularly bold idea. He would take the final scene of Goethe's great verse drama *Faust*, Part Two, in which Faust, who had previously sold his soul to the Devil, is absolved and redeemed by the Blessed Virgin Mary, and taken up into heaven. Immediately, Mahler began to note correspondences between the two texts. When the Virgin appears, she urges her fellow heavenly beings with the words: 'Komm! hebe dich zu höhren Sphären! / Wenn er dich ahnet, folgt er nach' ('Come! Raise yourself to higher spheres! / When he senses you, he will follow you').

The key word 'Komm' parallels the Latin hymn's opening *Veni*, which also means 'come'. More importantly, both texts dwell on the central importance of redeeming love, one of Mahler's lifelong preoccupations. The 'love' described in the Latin hymn is pure, not earthly but divine, while Goethe's concept fully embraces the erotic. But this was not a source of tension for Mahler. In a letter to Alma dated 18 June 1910 he finds a link in the much-misunderstood (then as much as now) concept of 'Platonic love', as described by the Ancient Greek philosopher Plato in his *Symposium*. The essence of true Platonic love, Mahler says...

> ...[is] Goethe's belief that all love is founded not only of the body but also of the soul, and that the two together constitute an outlet for this 'eros'. In the closing scene of Faust the concept is represented symbolically. The surface attraction of the Symposium lies in the vitality of its narrative and the dramatic fire of its 'story'... Only later does one appreciate the diversity of opinions proffered, and only at the very end does one realize what this carefully planned rise in intensity is actually leading to: that wonderful dialogue between Socrates and Diotima, in which Plato outlines and summarizes his entire world... One is tempted to compare him to Jesus Christ... Eros in both cases as the creator of the world!

Many of the Eighth Symphony's intellectual and emotional threads are drawn together in that letter. Platonic love, Christ and Goethe's redeeming *Ewig-Weibliche* ('Eternal Feminine') are all manifestations of the same thing: the primal erotic love that creates the world. And when Mahler talks about the 'carefully planned rise in intensity' leading to a climax that 'outlines and summarizes [the] entire world', he could just as well have been describing the closing stages of his own vaultingly ambitious symphony: a hymn to love as creator and love as redeemer, and thereby, as the Eighth Symphony's dedication makes explicit, to his adored, complicated Alma.

In another letter to Alma, written in 1909, Mahler explains how the final lines of Goethe's poem are the unifying force behind the whole symphony. The words of Goethe's concluding 'Chorus mysticus' are: 'Alles Vergängliche / Ist nur ein Gleichnis; / Das Unzulängliche, / Hier wid's Ereignis; / Das Unbeschreibliche, / Hier ist's getan; / Das Ewig-Weibliche / Zieht uns hinan' ('Everything transient / is but an allegory; / the inadequate / is here achieved; / the inexpressible / is here accomplished; / the Eternal Feminine / leads us onwards').

Mahler drew the threads together in that letter to Alma, a letter strikingly full of underlinings, showing how deeply, passionately, he pondered the significance of Goethe's words:

> So everything here is an _allegory_ a means of expressing an idea, which is by definition _inadequate_ to fulfil the requirements. While it may be possible to describe _transient_ things, we can feel or imagine but never _approach_ what underlies them (all that which 'here is _achieved_'), for it is transcendental and unchanging, hence _inexpressible_. That which leads us forwards with mystical strength, which every creature, perhaps even every stone, knows with absolute certainty to be the center of its existence, and which Goethe here calls _The Eternal Feminine_. Here, too, _an allegory_, namely _a fixed point_, the _goal_ is the antithesis of eternal longing, striving, motion towards that goal, in a word the Eternal Masculine.

Central to it all, he tells Alma is the *love force*, the power that has given him the strength and vision to create the kind of symphony he described to Sibelius: the symphony that would be 'like the world' and thus 'embrace everything'.

With all that in mind, the Eighth Symphony's apparently indestructible nickname, 'Symphony of a Thousand', feels like a cheapening of Mahler's philosophical goals: as though all he were concerned with was creating a huge, self-proclaiming monument in sound. There is far more to the work than that. Undeniably part of the Eighth Symphony's impact lies in the way Mahler manipulates his vast vocal and instrumental forces: eight soloists, boys' choir, large double chorus, twenty-two woodwind, seventeen brass *plus* offstage brass ensemble, organ *and* harmonium, piano, celeste, harps, mandolin, percussion and large string orchestra. In fact some of the most telling moments in the symphony occur at moments of extreme delicacy, as though Mahler's purpose in assembling such huge numbers were the creation of an immense chamber orchestra. But the climaxes are glorious too, especially the very ending, in which all the symphony's leading musical motifs are drawn together in near-cataclysmic affirmation.

Yet there have been dissenting voices on the subject of the Eighth Symphony. For the controversial German philosopher-critic Theodor Adorno (1903–1969), the whole thing proved that ultimately 'Mahler is no yea-sayer', that he was more at home creating worlds of night, suffering and despair than in striving for light and redemption. The British composer and writer Robert Simpson praised Part One, but lamented the way that Part Two, as he put it, degenerated into 'an ocean of shameless kitsch'. The conductor Simon Rattle kept the Eighth till last when recording his Mahler cycle, because of his long-standing doubts about the work. When eventually Rattle did come to conduct the Eighth Symphony, it was with a performance that vindicated the work as a cohesive symphonic statement, and which at the same time showed how over-simple, how reductive Adorno's approach had been.

There are certainly concerns about Mahler's final overwhelming hymn to the redeeming *Mater Gloriosa* ('Glorious Mother'), but this doesn't necessarily make the music weaker. Some of the ecstatic outpourings of Part Two have a poignant 'too good to be true' quality; but in addition there are moments where the music itself registers a pain one would expect to have no place in heaven, even a quasi-pagan heaven. Just before the final magnificent crescendo, based on the words of Goethe's 'Chorus mysticus', there is a touching little interlude for solo piccolo, harmonium, celeste, piano and harps. It tinkles prettily like the star in the nursery rhyme, but then comes a darkening of the harmony (quiet muted brass) and a sad falling clarinet phrase. Just for a moment the expression changes, as though, between two great ecstatic waves of praise, Mahler had allowed a sigh of longing to escape.

A more serious criticism could be levelled at Mahler's word setting. This is not something that English-speaking listeners normally notice, but a great deal of the Goethe setting in Part Two is rhythmically much more four-square than the musical treatment of the Latin hymn in Part One. This was the only time in Mahler's composing career that he chose truly great German verse, and it may be because Goethe's rhythms are so strong in themselves that Mahler's settings sometimes seem a touch rhythmically inhibited, even wooden – a charge one would never level at the *Rückert Lieder* or *Das Lied von der Erde*. At the centre of Part Two comes one of Goethe's most famous lines, a saying that could have been written to describe Mahler himself: 'Wer immer strebend sich bemüht, / Den können wir erlösen' ('The man who will strive with all his might, / Him we can redeem'). One cannot help feeling that

Poster for the premiere of Mahler's Eighth Symphony in Munich, 1910

Mahler: *"Wie geht denn das zu, im Zuhörerraum ist keine einzige Katze?"*

Konzertveranstalter: *"Wo sollen die denn herkommen? Wir brauchen ja jeden Schwanz zur Aufführung!"*

Mahler misses an opportunity here, a chance to make that great saying entirely his own.

Mahler, however, thought the Eighth to be the finest of his symphonies, and its first performance in Munich in September 1910 brought him the greatest triumph of his life, both as conductor and composer: a success that he had striven for, despaired of, and striven for again through decades.

Crisis at the Opera

While the years 1905 and 1906 were fantastically productive on the composition front, at the same time Mahler was finding life at the Vienna Opera more and more of a drain on his creative resources. The praise continued, but there were still the old grumbles from some quarters about his typically 'free' attitude to tempo and about his re-orchestrations of the sacred masters. Added to these were growing complaints that he was now spending too much time away from his post, conducting his own music. Writing from Frankfurt in January

1907, Mahler said that he felt like 'a hunted stag, the hounds in full cry'. This was partly occasioned by a series of bad reviews of his own works. He also told Alma exasperatedly that: 'All the newspapers have reports from Vienna of my resignation. Does it mean that there is another outcry because of my prolonged absence? The newspapers say that I have piled up an enormous deficit, that I have become impossible, etc. etc.'

The last charge must have stung. Expenditure had indeed risen at the Opera, but that was as a result of Mahler's drive for perfection (the cost of Roller's ground-breaking

Mahler and Alma in Rome, 1907

designs, for one thing). More worryingly, box-office takings had fallen. Mahler now had plenty of enemies, especially in the overtly anti-Semitic sections of the Viennese press (one critic had labelled him 'the Jewish dwarf'), and behind the scenes others were taking advantage of the controversy, plotting and spreading gossip. Mahler's relationship with the Court Chamberlain, Prince Montenuovo, previously friendly and respectful on both sides, deteriorated. On 31 March 1907 Mahler handed in his resignation. But was this quite the 'blow of fate' that Alma describes in *Memories and Letters*? Was Mahler 'forced' to resign as a result of the growing campaign against him? Partly, perhaps, but there is plenty of evidence that Mahler was increasingly tired of the huge effort involved in both conducting and directing opera. As early as 1905 he had told Natalie Bauer-Lechner: 'I should like best to live only for my compositions and, to tell the truth, I am beginning to neglect my operatic duties.' In 1906 he wrote to Natalie as though his mind were already made up:

> All things have their day and I have had mine and so has my work as the local opera director... So I want to go at a point when I can still expect that, at a later date, the Viennese will learn to appreciate what I did for their theatre.

Mahler may well have decided that the best policy was to 'quit while you're ahead', in which case one could argue that it worked. Mahler's reign at the Vienna Opera did eventually come to be seen as its Golden Age, and many of those who took up arms against him at the time came, as Mahler prophesied, to regret their decision. There were other frustrations too. Mahler was angered by the Court authorities' refusal to sanction performances of Strauss's controversial new opera *Salome*. The conservative censors in this still staunchly Roman Catholic city took strong exception to the work's 'decadent' eroticizing of the story of St John the Baptist's execution. Mahler had been hugely impressed by *Salome*: 'a live volcano, a subterranean fire, one of the greatest masterpieces of our time' was his verdict. He sent off a coruscating letter to Strauss, bitterly lamenting the hidebound attitudes that had prevented him from performing it. Half-affectionately, Strauss rebuked Mahler for taking his duties at the Vienna Opera too seriously: 'A pigsty that wouldn't even perform *Salome*. Not worth it I tell you.' Deep in his heart, Mahler must have agreed.

Mahler's reign at the Vienna Opera did eventually come to be seen as its Golden Age, and many of those who took up arms against him at the time came, as Mahler prophesied, to regret their decision.

In any case Mahler was being courted from another direction: America. Heinrich Conried, Manager of New York's Metropolitan Opera House, had been impressed by what he had heard about Mahler. Conried knew he needed a star conductor to beat off competition from New York's newly established Manhattan Opera House. Before long he had formed the resolution that Mahler was the man to do the job, and that he must be engaged at all costs. Conried approached Mahler well before his resignation in 1907. He offered a huge salary, more than double what Mahler earned in Vienna, and there was an added attraction in that he would be required only as music director: staging, direction, costumes and so forth would be taken care of by others. Having left his mark on the world of opera production, Mahler seems to have been only too happy to let someone else take the reins. So despite a massive public declaration of support from many of most famous names in artistic Vienna, Mahler decided to leave Vienna for the New World and a better-paid job, one that might allow him more time and energy for composing. Alma records one of Mahler's remarks as they set off together for New York at the end of 1907:

> 'Repertory opera is done with,' Mahler observed during the journey. 'I'm glad not to be staying on to witness its decline. Up to the last I contrived to hide from the public that I was making bricks without straw.'

Bearing all that in mind, it becomes harder to credit Alma's contention that Mahler's departure from Vienna was a catastrophic, 'forced' decision, a 'blow of fate'.

Alma mentioned two other blows of fate that befell Mahler in 1907. In one case at least, the effect was immediate and devastating.

Chapter 8

Catastrophe

Catastrophe

At the beginning of the summer of 1907 Mahler set off as usual for his composing holiday at Maiernigg, but a few days after his arrival came a terrible shock. His much loved Putzi developed scarlet fever and diptheria. Soon Gucki too was showing signs of the same dangerous sickness. Gucki eventually recovered; Putzi did not, despite desperate attempts to save her, including an attempted tracheotomy. Alma's description in *Memories and Letters* is especially painful to read:

> We passed a fortnight in an agony of dread; there was a relapse and the danger of suffocation. It was a ghastly time, accompanied by thunderstorms and lurid skies. Mahler loved this child devotedly; he hid himself in his room every day, taking leave of her in his heart. On the last night, when a tracheotomy was resorted to, I posted his servant at his door to keep him in his room if the noise disturbed him; but he slept all through this terrible night. My English nurse and I got the operation table ready and put the poor child to sleep. When the operation was being performed I ran along the shore of the lake, where no one could hear me crying. The doctor had forbidden me to enter the room; and at five in the morning the nurse came to tell me it was over. Then I saw her. She lay

choking, with her large eyes wide open. Our agony dragged on one more whole day. Then the end came.

Mahler, weeping and sobbing, went again and again to the door of my bedroom, where she was; then fled away to be out of earshot of any sound. It was more than he could bear. We telegraphed to my mother, who came at once. We all slept in his room. We could not bear being parted for an hour. We dreaded what might happen if we left the room. We were like birds in a storm and feared what each moment might bring – and how right we were.

There was indeed more to come. As Putzi's coffin was placed on the hearse, Alma's mother had a heart attack. Alma herself fell into a deep faint. The doctor was summoned again. Then, Alma says, the second 'blow of fate' fell:

Mahler thinking to make a cheerful diversion and distract us from our gloom said: 'Come along, doctor, wouldn't you like to examine me too?' The doctor did so. He got up, looking very serious. Mahler was lying on the sofa and Dr Blumenthal had been kneeling beside him. 'Well, you've no cause to be proud of a heart like that,' he said in the cheery tone doctors often adopt after diagnosing a fatal disease. This verdict meant the beginning of the end for Mahler... [He] went to Vienna by the next train to consult Professor Kovacs, who fully confirmed the verdict of the general practitioner: hereditary, though compensated, valve defects on both sides.

Some writers have suggested that Alma made too much of this diagnosis. The heart defect was, after all, 'compensated'. Things might well have been manageable if Mahler had taken care of himself. The doctor prescribed a new regime: no more mountain climbing, cycling or swimming. Walking was possible, but Mahler had to be gradually reintroduced to it: five minutes at first, then ten, then more. The idea of taking care, of relaxing his habitually strenuous lifestyle, must have been dreadful for Mahler, the composer who derived so much inspiration from energetic walks and, later, cycling. Still, when he went for his inoculation in Vienna later in 1907, Mahler was able to report the specialist's verdict cheerfully: 'It's funny, but in substance he said just what Blumenthal said, but his whole way of saying it was somehow reassuring.' He remembered how his mother had gone for years 'at full speed' despite her similar heart problem. In certain moods at least, Mahler does not seem to have taken this 'fateful' diagnosis as a death sentence, or even as a sign that he should have to change his habits permanently.

Towards Eternity: Das Lied von der Erde

Almost certainly the impact of that catastrophic summer in 1907 left an imprint on his next major work. A spiritual fault-line separates Mahler's *Das Lied von der Erde* ('The Song of the Earth', 1907–9) from his previous major composition, the Eighth Symphony. While they are obviously the work of the same composer, you have only to compare their endings to realize how much had changed in Mahler's world-view. The Eighth Symphony concludes in massive, radiant affirmation: not only are life and love eternal, but they will lead the striving soul 'ever onwards'. *Das Lied von der Erde* also ends with a vision of eternity: 'Everywhere the dear Earth blossoms in spring and grows green again'; but now the artist himself stands painfully apart from this eternal renewal: 'I seek rest for my lonely heart! I journey homewards, to my resting-place. I shall never again seek the far distance. My heart is still and awaits its hour!' Note the significant repetitions of the word 'heart'.

As Mahler struggled to recover from the events of 1907, it does seem to have been the state of his health that worried him increasingly, although this could well be an example of what psychologists call 'transference anxiety': health worries resorted to as a distraction from a deeper underlying pain (the loss of Putzi). The following summer, as he turned again to thoughts of composing, Mahler wrote to Bruno Walter:

> I must alter my whole way of life. You cannot imagine how painful this is for me. For years I have grown used to taking strenuous exercise, to walking in forests and over mountains and boldly wresting my ideas from nature... Now I must avoid all effort, watch myself constantly, walk as little as possible.

Walter tried to challenge Mahler by implying that his problems were more psychological than physical. Mahler was unimpressed:

> I have in no sense a hypochondriac's fear of death, as you suppose. I have always known that I must die... But as far as my work is concerned, it is most depressing to have to unlearn everything. I have never been able to compose only at my desk. I need outside exercise for my inner exercises... After a gentle little walk my pulse beats so fast and I feel so oppressed that I don't even achieve the desired effect of forgetting my body... This is the greatest calamity I have ever known.

The increased pulse and 'oppressed' feelings could just as easily have been a symptom of grief as a sign that Mahler's heart had become significantly weaker, as Walter sensed; but for Mahler the feeling was real enough, whatever the cause.

Yet, out of this calamity came what for many is Mahler's most perfect achievement: his 'song-symphony' *Das Lied von der Erde*. After the terrible events of the summer of

1907, both Mahler and Alma appear to have agreed that life at Maiernigg was no longer possible. There were too many dreadful associations. So the 'Villa Mahler' was abandoned, and the family fled to Schluderbach in the Tyrol. Here Mahler seems to have revived a little, and took walks again, though not as strenuously as before. It was here that he was given a copy of *Die chinesische Flöte* ('The Chinese Flute') by, according to Alma, 'an old consumptive friend of my father's, who transferred all the love he had for him to Mahler': curious that Alma withheld his name.

Die chinesische Flöte is a collection of poems by Hans Bethge (1876–1946) based on translations of ancient Chinese texts. Mahler found much in Bethge's verse that spoke directly to him or, as Alma put it, 'their infinite melancholy answered to his own'. Again and again the poems tell of an almost painfully intense feeling for the beauty of life on earth and a poignant sense of how fleeting is man's part in it. In several of them he found reflected the heightened loneliness he had felt since the onset of the crisis. One can well imagine what Mahler would have made of the frequent references to the heart itself, not just in the closing lines of the final song, but still more tellingly in the second movement, **'Der Einsame im Herbst'** ('The Lonely One in Autumn'): 'My heart is weary. My little lamp burns out with a sputter; it puts me in mind of sleep'. There are also searing expressions of bitterness, especially in the first song, 'Das Trinklied vom Jammer der Erde' ('The Drinking Song of the Earth's Misery'), in which the poet desperately seeks release from thoughts of death through alcohol, a theme Mahler returns to in the fifth movement, 'Der Trunkene im Frühling' ('The Drunkard in Spring'). Excessive drinking was never a weakness to which Mahler was prone; these two songs are an important reminder that not everything in his work is directly autobiographical.

CD 2
track 6

www.naxosbooks.com

If *Das Lied von der Erde* were all bitterness, pain, horror and loneliness, it would not be the widely loved work that it is. Some have found its message bleak and pessimistic, but the composer Benjamin Britten (1913 –1976) spoke for many when he described the ending as having 'a serenity literally supernatural'. In the poems there are glimmers of hope: particularly the possibility of an acceptance that brings peace. Mahler intensified these not only in his music, but in the lines that he altered or added. The final words of the last song, 'Der Abschied' ('The Farewell'), are Mahler's own. Those critics who condemn Mahler as 'egoistic' should consider that this is perhaps the least self-centred utterance in the entire work: 'Die liebe Erde allüberall blüht auf im Lenze und grünt aufs neu! / Allüberall und ewig blauen licht die Fernen! / Ewig... Ewig...' ('The dear earth everywhere blossoms in spring and grows green again! / Everywhere and eternally the distance shines bright and blue! / Eternally... Eternally...')

> As for the music, here Mahler's innovatory brilliance reaches its zenith. The orchestral writing in *Das Lied von der Erde* has a beauty that surpasses almost anything he had written before.

Life goes on, the earth constantly renews itself, whether the artist is there to see it or not. Joy is mixed with, and perhaps even transcends, personal regret. Significantly, the closing 'Chorus mysticus' of the Eighth Symphony had also made great play with repetitions of the word 'Ewig' ('Eternally'); but here the effect is utterly different: quiet acceptance replaces massive affirmation.

As for the music, here Mahler's innovatory brilliance reaches its zenith. For Mahler the artist, a heightened intensity of feeling in the face of death ('I am thirstier than ever for life,' he wrote) was a spur to new creative heights. The orchestral writing in *Das Lied von der Erde* has a beauty that surpasses almost anything he had written before. Even more than in any earlier work Mahler creates a unique world of sound, not so much in colors as through vivid musical images that fix themselves in the memory: the weirdly fluttering flutes and rasping low trombone chords in the first song, accompanying the nightmare image of the ape in the graveyard; the frail, spare lines of the second, 'Der Einsame im Herbst'; the hollow, deep bell sounds that open 'Der Abschied'; and the floating, dissolving, almost timeless textures that surround the singer's slowly fading 'Ewig... Ewig...' at the end – perhaps the most truly visionary music in all of Mahler's output. We could hardly be further from the somewhat wooden regularity of the word setting that occasionally mars Part Two of the Eighth Symphony. Not only does the vocal line seem to float sublimely in the closing pages, intoxicated by the sound of the words, but the orchestral writing is the most rhythmically complex Mahler ever created – yet the effect is of ecstatic improvisatory freedom.

Mahler's use of the device known as 'heterophony' (where instruments play more or less the same lines but at different speeds) suggests that he may well have looked seriously at Chinese 'classical' music; if so, the sounds he distils from it are utterly his own. In general, Mahler's orchestral *chinoiserie* goes way beyond the conventional 'exotic' kitsch of the time. One may be able to pick out oriental details: the use of pentatonic melodies (as though played only on the 'black notes' of the piano) or of interweaving mandolin, celeste and harps to evoke the sounds of Chinese courtly orchestras. In much of this Mahler seems to look far beyond his own time, to the music of the second half of the twentieth century.

New World, New Hopes?

It is possible that, as well as looking forward musically, Mahler was beginning to view his own future with something closer to hope, especially as the date for the planned departure for New York approached. Alma's account of their setting off, in December 1907, manages to suggest a qualified optimism:

> *The moment of our departure arrived. Schoenberg and Zemlinsky marshalled their pupils and Mahler's friends on the platform, to which they had been given private access. They were all drawn up when we arrived, flowers in their hands and tears in their eyes, ready to board the train and deck our compartment with flowers from roof to floor. When we drew slowly out it was without regret or backward glances. We had been too hard hit. All we wanted was to get away, the farther the better. We even felt happy as Vienna was left behind. We did not miss our child, who had been left behind with my mother. We knew now that anxious love was no avail against catastrophe, and that no spot on earth gives immunity. We had been through the fire. So we thought. But in spite of all, one thing had us in its grip: the future.*

So, while Mahler and his wife had both been 'hard hit', they were now full of thoughts of 'the future'. This is a different Mahler from the one who, according to Alma, had sensed 'the beginning of the end' only a few months before. When attempting to assess the message contained in Mahler's last works this must be borne in mind. Almost certainly there were times when he felt that *Das Lied von der Erde* or either of the two symphonies that followed might turn out to be his own 'Farewell'. Particularly strong evidence for that exists in the case of the Ninth Symphony; but there is also evidence that Mahler, in other moods, might have seen this whole horrendous episode as a 'dark night of the soul' – one to be endured, and perhaps also outlived: a trial by fire that may yet lead to better things.

Interestingly, this is how a significant number of writers and conductors have chosen to view the Tenth Symphony.

Farewell to Life? The Ninth Symphony

When *Das Lied von der Erde* and Mahler's last completed symphony, the Ninth (1909–10), were heard for the first time, in the year following Mahler's death, many listeners were struck by the works' intense preoccupation with mortality. It was highlighted in the texts of *Das Lied von der Erde*, and clear enough in the expressive tone of the Ninth Symphony, especially in its *Adagio* finale. The composer Alban Berg (1885–1935), who revered Mahler, described the Ninth Symphony's first movement as 'the expression of an exceptional fondness for this earth, the longing to live in peace on it, to enjoy nature to its depths before death comes. For he comes irresistibly. The whole movement is permeated with premonitions of death.' Then, of course, those first audiences had the benefit of hindsight. That Mahler suffered from heart problems had become well known in musical Vienna. Speculation soon became certainty: Mahler must have known that he was going to die, and the Ninth Symphony was therefore his 'Farewell to Life', the title Bruckner had given to the last movement of his own (incomplete) Ninth Symphony.

> Speculation soon became certainty: Mahler must have known that he was going to die, and the Ninth Symphony was therefore his 'Farewell to Life'.

There are good reasons to be wary about accepting this reading unconditionally. Mahler may have been shaken by the diagnosis of his heart problem, but it wasn't until the very last year of his life that he began to slacken the pace of his frantically busy professional life. In 1909, two years after the ominous diagnosis, he accepted a three-year contract to conduct the New York Philharmonic Orchestra (his first season included an astonishing forty-six concerts). Then in 1910 Mahler began, and very nearly finished, a Tenth Symphony, another ambitious orchestral work, leading to a very different conclusion from that expressed in the closing pages of Symphony No. 9.

If the idea of mortality does haunt the pages of his Ninth Symphony, this does not necessarily mean that Mahler was thinking exclusively of his own end. In the symphony's final bars, before the music yields completely to silence, there is that significant quotation in the violins from the final lyrical phrase of the fourth of the *Kindertotenlieder*, associated with the words: 'We'll find them again on the heights in sunshine! The day is beautiful on those heights.' Was Mahler thinking of his own death here, or that of his favorite daughter Putzi, and perhaps also of his dead brothers Ernst and Otto? Whatever the inspiration, this would not be the first time that Mahler had imaginatively 'lived through' the experience of death in his music (other examples being the funeral marches in the First, Second and Fifth symphonies and *Lieder eines fahrenden Gesellen*, or the ending of the Sixth Symphony). As early as 1879, when just nineteen years old, Mahler had written to a friend a letter that was already full of not just the sentiments but even some of the very words he later put into music in *Das Lied von der Erde*: 'Oh my beloved earth, when, oh when, will you take the forsaken one to your breast? Behold, mankind has banished him from itself, and he flees from its cold and heartless bosom to you, to you! Oh care for the lonely one, the restless one, Universal Mother!'

The language may be touched with romantic convention, but the sentiments were real enough. The diagnosis of the heart weakness may have given his thoughts a new urgency, for a while at least, but it only magnified what was already there. When Berg wrote of the presence of death in the

Ninth Symphony, he was not simply giving voice to a fanciful personal interpretation: the music is full of details that reinforce his words.

From very early on, the first movement is dominated by a two-note falling figure, like a sigh (first heard in the second violins). In the finale this figure returns, but it now falls by two steps, clearly spelling out the leading motif from Beethoven's Piano Sonata 'Les Adieux', the work that Mahler had played to such great effect in his teens. Beethoven marked this motif 'Le-be-wohl' ('Farewell') in his manuscript, a fact of which Mahler would have been well aware. In the first movement of Mahler's Ninth the two-note sighing version of the 'Farewell' motif emerges after a short introduction, in which cellos and low horn spell out a strange, faltering rhythm (the conductor and composer Leonard Bernstein compared this to Mahler's heightened awareness of his own heartbeat). The exquisite, long violin melody that grows from the first sighing figures returns many times during the course of this long first movement. Contrasted episodes between its appearances are by turn impassioned, frantic, resigned and eerie. One passage, introduced by the 'faltering heart' rhythm on horns, followed by sinister drum taps, is unmistakably a funeral march. Towards the end of the movement comes a sinister, skeletally scored episode, in which Mahler treats his large orchestra as though it were a much smaller chamber ensemble. It is as if the orchestra itself were fragmenting, breaking down. But it is the sense of the sweetness of life that prevails in the final bars, the orchestration wonderfully delicate and imaginative to the very last note, magically scored for piccolo, harp and string harmonics.

The second movement is a surprise, every bit as

But it is the sense of the sweetness of life that prevails in the final bars, the orchestration wonderfully delicate and imaginative to the very last note.

dislocating as the sudden change of mood at the beginning of the Fifth Symphony's scherzo. Suddenly the listener is transported to an Austrian beer-garden, with coarse, heavy-footed dance tunes. In fact three kinds of Ländler alternate in this movement: the 'leisurely' first theme, a faster, more boisterous dance tune (becoming positively thuggish later on), and a gentle, sentimental slow waltz, leading off with a return of the first movement's two-note 'sigh'. Comical though much of this music is, it has a disquieting air, especially in the coda, where the character of the first Ländler tune turns dark and grotesque.

All this is brusquely thrust aside by the rondo (or 'Burleske', as Mahler subtitled it). Brilliantly, sometimes garishly, scored, this is the movement in which Mahler shows off his contrapuntal skills with splendid panache. A lot of this music has a sarcastic tone, confirmed by Mahler's dedication of this movement 'To my brothers in Apollo' – a raspberry directed at the musical pedants who had found fault with his contrapuntal techniques. So again there is a possible point of contact with Mahler's Fifth Symphony, whose finale began with another joke at his critics' expense. Intriguingly, the overall tonal scheme of the Ninth Symphony is an almost exact reversal of that of No. 5. The Fifth Symphony progresses from a death-haunted C sharp minor to a strenuously optimistic D major; the Ninth begins in D major, but falls in the *Adagio* finale to D flat major / C sharp minor. And just as the Fifth's final triumphant D major is anticipated, briefly, at the end of its second movement, so the Ninth's rondo 'Burleske' gives one wistful glance back at the D major in which it began. This occurs at the heart of the movement in an extraordinary bitter-sweet episode, introduced by a sugary slow tune on a solo trumpet. It seems to aspire to higher things, but aspiration comes to nothing, with mocking sneers from high clarinets.

The energetic counterpoint resumes, and the movement ends as it began, full of sound and fury.

Finally comes the *Adagio*. In placing the symphony's slow movement last, Mahler may have been thinking of Tchaikovsky's 'Pathétique' Symphony (1893) or of Bruckner's Ninth, both of which were overshadowed by thoughts of death. The intensely expressive rising violin figure that begins this movement strongly recalls the opening of Bruckner's concluding *Adagio,* but what Mahler achieves is utterly personal. The first theme on full strings spells out Beethoven's 'Farewell' theme in full, and there is also a striking echo of the Victorian funeral hymn *Abide with me.* The resemblance may be coincidental, but it is possible that Mahler heard the hymn during his time in New York. This richly sonorous music alternates with weird, sparsely scored passages: more skeletal sounds, even more 'broken down' than in the chamber-like passage near the end of the first movement. Eventually, the 'Farewell' theme builds to a massive, desperate climax, which seems to be striving for the transcendent glory of the Eighth Symphony. There is even a quotation from the great closing hymn of the Eighth: horns sing out the motif, which in the Eighth is associated with the words 'Ewig, Ewig' ('Eternally, Eternally'), but in this context the sentiment seems shorn of hope. The striving is in vain, and the rich textures gradually thin out into the near-emptiness of the final bars; the silences between the slow, quiet phrases are almost unbearably poignant, like the pauses between the breaths of a dying man. At last the music fades into nothingness: the final chord is marked 'esterbend' (literally 'dying away'). Mahler may not have given up on life just yet, but the end of the Ninth Symphony shows just how much he must have thought of

At last the music fades into nothingness: the final chord is marked 'esterbend' (literally 'dying away').

death in the years following that catastrophic last summer at
Maiernigg.

'A Frightful Confession'

Mahler's work on *Das Lied von der Erde* and the Ninth
Symphony occupied a number of years. He may have left
Vienna in December 1907 with hopes for the future, but
within a few years he was to be engulfed in storms of a different
kind, which this time related directly to his relationship with
Alma. It is said that the death of a child has destroyed many
a marriage. Alma and Gustav Mahler were still together, but
the loss of Putzi and Mahler's increased concentration on his
own problems, real or exaggerated, had evidently begun to
drive a wedge between them. When the Mahlers arrived in
France, prior to their embarkation for America, they were
met by a friend, the young Russian pianist and conductor
Ossip Gabrilovitch. With impressive candor, Alma relates
what happened next:

> *Our friend Gabrilovitch, who worshipped Mahler blindly,*
> *awaited us in Paris. He and I were alone that evening. He*
> *blurted out: 'I have a frightful confession to make. I'm on*
> *the verge of falling in love with you. Help me to get over it.*
> *I love Mahler. I could not bear to hurt him.' I was too dazed*
> *to speak. So I was capable of arousing love: I was not old*
> *and ugly, as I had come to think. He felt for my hand in*
> *the dark. The light was switched on and Mahler came in;*
> *he was affectionate and kindly and the specter vanished.*
> *Nevertheless, this episode was my standby for some time in*
> *many an onset of self-deprecation.*

For all Mahler's outpourings of love for Alma, she still felt 'old and ugly'; she was only twenty-eight, and Mahler's apparent innocence over the possibility that anything significant had taken place between Alma and Gabrilovitch is both symptomatic and worrying. Alma's determination to put her husband and his art first, whatever her private feelings, and the experience at Maiernigg of being sidelined, condemned to the role of childminder, had left her feeling more than ever like a bird with clipped wings. Her diaries (frank as ever) make it clear that, physically speaking, Mahler was never very satisfying as a lover. Now a young man professes his love and the effect is like dropping a match into dry tinder. On this occasion nothing came of it; but the next time the consequences would be disastrous.

Chapter 9

'To Live for You, To Die for You'

'To Live for You, To Die for You'

For generations of Mahler lovers, the Ninth Symphony was, in effect, Mahler's last work. No wonder then that its 'Farewell' message was widely taken to be a premonition of his own fast-approaching end. Thanks to the efforts of devoted Mahlerians like Deryck Cooke and, earlier, Joe Wheeler, we now know that this was not the end of the story. Cooke in particular was able to show the world that the tortuous, sometimes near-indecipherable mass of sketches for the Tenth Symphony could be read and understood. More importantly, they showed that the Tenth was more or less complete in Mahler's mind when he died. One movement, the opening *Adagio*, is virtually filled out in orchestral score, while the others survive either as four-stave sketch scores (like a piano-duet version) or in partly orchestrated full scores. As Cooke, Wheeler and others have demonstrated, a great deal of important information can be inferred from these sketches even when Mahler is not specific about harmonies, counter-melodies or orchestral colors. When one compares the various attempts to provide what Deryck Cooke called 'a performing version' of these sketches it is strikingly obvious that, despite differences in detail here and there, in broader terms they are all recognizably the same symphony. Gradually, Cooke's version has won more and more converts. When Simon Rattle performed and recorded the score in Berlin in 1999, even some of the staunchly resistant German critics dropped their defences and admitted that it not only sounded like Mahler, it sounded like very good Mahler. When taking the Tenth Symphony into account, the story of Mahler's last years, artistically speaking, has a rather different complexion. Amazingly, the Tenth Symphony seems to begin where the Ninth left off: hushed and awestruck in the presence of death but eventually, after enduring further tribulations and arriving at a vision of final extinction even more terrifying than anything in the Ninth, it works through to a very different, more positive conclusion. It could well be that Mahler thought the danger of imminent death was past, for the moment at least, and that he could now look forward to exploring new musical paths. The Tenth Symphony is full of fascinating pointers to possible ways ahead.

> When taking the Tenth Symphony into account, the story of Mahler's last years, artistically speaking, has a rather different complexion.

'Making' Mahler: New York

That Mahler's last symphony ultimately seems to hold out the possibility of renewed hope may be partly a reflection of his experiences in the New World. Once installed at The Metropolitan Opera, Mahler was as incapable as ever of taking things easy, at least when it came to his workload. Despite their efforts to put the past behind them, Alma records that she was tormented by memories of Maria and her dreadful end. Her free time (she had a great deal of that) hung heavily upon her. She recalls with horror an occasion where, at some New York society gathering, they were both introduced to a raddled old actress who also bore the nickname 'Putzi'. It was too much. Excuses were made, and the Mahlers left hurriedly. Mahler himself, on the other hand, seems to have been trying

Mahler in New York, 1910

to bury his feelings about his lost daughter in his work at The Metropolitan – perhaps in an effort to keep grief at bay until he again had time to work it out through music. At the same time, both Alma and Mahler were fascinated by what they found in America. In the midst of her accounts of loneliness and insomnia, Alma also describes New York as 'this divine city': more proof that she shared something of her husband's propensity for extreme mood-swings.

Mahler was thrilled to discover that he would make his Metropolitan Opera debut with Wagner's *Tristan und Isolde*, still for him one of the very highest peaks of German opera and a work of special personal significance. Mahler conducted *Tristan* on New Year's Day 1908. The critics were generally positive: 'The influence of the new conductor was felt and heard in the whole spirit of the performance,' enthused the *New York Times*. 'Through it all went the pulse of dramatic beauty.' Mahler was further delighted by the quality of the singers. In New York he appeared to have lost some of his former terrifying determination, and Bruno Walter reports that Mahler's conducting style had relaxed somewhat; his

Caricatures of Mahler conducting, by Boehler

bodily movements were no longer those of an 'electrified cat', as one Viennese critic had put it.

There were signs that Gustav and Alma Mahler were growing a little closer again. They enjoyed sharing the typical European wry reactions to the bizarre eccentricities and fantasies indulged in by so many rich Americans: the kind of unselfconscious extravagance that would later produce the great Hollywood spectaculars or the taste-defying fantasy world of the millionaire Randolph Hearst's 'Hearst Castle'. If Mahler had lived longer and stayed in America, one wonders whether he might have discovered a *métier* for writing film music, like another great Austrian émigré, Erich Wolfgang Korngold (1897–1957). It is certain, however, that Mahler's sense of the ironic would have been hard to silence. This too was something Alma shared with him. Her account of their introductory lunch with The Metropolitan Opera's director, Heinrich Conried, is deliciously wicked:

> **If Mahler had lived longer and stayed in America, one wonders whether he might have discovered a *métier* for writing film music.**

Andreas Dippel, who was then business manager of The Metropolitan, took us to lunch with the super-god, Conried, who was already a cripple from tabes and showed unmistakable signs of megalomania. This first, fantastic luncheon party, the flat itself and our hosts' utter innocence of culture, kept us in concealed mirth until we were in the street again and could burst out laughing. In Conried's smoking-room, for example, there was a suit of armour which could be illuminated from within by red lights. There was a divan in the middle of the room with a baldacchino and convoluted pillars, and on it the godlike Conried reclined when he gave audience to the members of the company. All was enveloped, somber, flounced stuffs, illuminated by the glare of colored electric lights. And

> *then, Conried himself, who had 'made' Sonnenthal and was*
> *now going to 'make' Mahler.*

On the whole, work at The Metropolitan Opera went more smoothly than it had in Vienna. Of course, Mahler was now responsible only for the musical content, and he found that a huge relief. There was no more arguing with Court chamberlains, no more criticism for extravagant spending to fend off. While in Vienna he took huge pains to bring the general standards of the production up to the level of the music-making; in New York he hardly seems to have minded that Conried's sets matched his taste in home décor. When the orchestra and the singers were so good, and so responsive to his conducting, it must hardly have mattered.

New Intrigues and a New Contract

This period of relative professional peace could not go on for ever. Before long, more politicking broke out at The Metropolitan. The flashpoint came when the services of a dazzlingly talented, energetic, slightly younger Italian conductor named Arturo Toscanini (1867–1957) were also engaged. One of The Metropolitan's leading financial backers, realizing that Conried's health was in serious decline, and that his days there were numbered, had approached Giulio Gatti-Casazza, director of La Scala Opera House in Milan, in the hope that he might take over when, inevitably, Conried resigned. Gatti-Casazza said 'yes', on the condition that Toscanini came with him. Toscanini made the right kind of political noises: 'I hold Mahler in very high esteem,' he told the board, but Mahler's suspicions mounted when Gatti-Casazza insisted, in February 1909, that Toscanini should conduct the next Metropolitan performance of *Tristan*. Mahler wrote indignantly to associate director Andreas Dippel:

> *It is inconceivable to me that a new production of* Tristan
> *should be put on without my being consulted in any way and*
> *I cannot give my consent... If recently, out of consideration for*
> *the wishes of my colleague* [Toscanini], *I gave a free hand to*
> *the new director, it was with the express exception of* Tristan.
> *I took very special pains with* Tristan *last season and can well*
> *maintain that the form in which this work now appears in*
> *New York is my spiritual property.*

For the moment Mahler got his way, but he now seemed to have lost his appetite for sustained battle campaigns. When a group of women supporters of the New York Philharmonic Society approached Mahler to see if he was interested in becoming the orchestra's conductor, they found him responsive. Granted, the orchestra was not on good form (having lost some of its best players to The Metropolitan) but the salary offered was excellent, and Mahler had no qualms about the 'hiring and firing' that would be necessary to restore it to top quality. It gave him the opportunity he had long wanted to promote important orchestral works by contemporary composers (including Richard Strauss), and it might help to solve a problem that had been at the back of Mahler's mind for some time. Although his own works were being performed more frequently, he was worried about the kind of performing traditions that might be attached to his music if he were unable to lead by example. In 1909, therefore, Mahler signed up for a three-year contract with the New York Philharmonic.

There were soon signs that the strain of struggling to form a new orchestra from the somewhat tattered remnants of an old one was proving too much for him. At one point in 1908

Alma recorded that Mahler was 'in excellent health', but now it seemed that his condition was beginning to deteriorate. When another hammer blow of fate hit him in 1910, he would not be in the best condition to survive it. Despite her enthusiasm for New York, Alma too had been showing signs of severe strain. The death of Putzi continued to haunt her, and she often found life in New York draining. There was also the problem of coping with Mahler's new regimes and the vicissitudes of his career: again, she felt sidelined at times. The experience with Gabrilovitch in Paris had heightened awareness of her long-term sexual frustration. Despite Mahler's reputation as a lothario, Alma describes his sexual performance as 'inexperienced'. There is a particularly painful account in Alma's diaries of the couple's first failed attempt at sex, and she gives the impression that there was no great improvement with time. It was not just the sex. Mahler was constantly involved in his own work and the exploration of his own inner world, and this capacity for self-absorption and self-dramatization made him a great artist but possibly a poor husband. Even when he was not actually working, Mahler was often conserving his physical energy, mindful of his heart problem. All Alma's old grievances resurfaced: Mahler had clipped her wings. She needed love, admiration, recognition of her own talents, not a self-preoccupied older man who still tended to patronize her or treat her as an ancillary to his genius. Mahler's idea of a pleasant family evening, she writes, was for her to read him serious German literature or philosophy. She bitterly recalled the remark made by a friend: 'You have an abstraction for a husband.'

> Mahler was constantly involved in his own work and the exploration of his own inner world, and this made him a great artist but possibly a poor husband.

175

Marital Crisis: Walter Gropius

In the summer of 1910, while Mahler set off to compose at his new retreat at Toblach in the Dolomites, Alma headed for a sanatorium in the Alpine spa town of Tobelbad. There the doctor she consulted diagnosed depression, almost certainly correctly, and prescribed a regime for her which he hoped would lift her spirits. It did, but for reasons that the good doctor may not have foreseen. In the first version of her memoirs, entitled *And the Bridge is Love*, Alma takes up the story thus:

> *The German doctor in charge of the place prescribed dancing! Well, it made more sense than the boiling baths. Feeling responsible for me and worried by my despondency and loneliness, he introduced young men to me; one was an extraordinary handsome German who would have been well cast as Walther von Stolzing in* Die Meistersinger.
>
> *We danced. Gliding slowly around the room with the youth, I heard that he was an architect and had studied with one of my father's well-known friends. We stopped dancing and talked.*
>
> *Soon there remained no doubt that young Walter Gropius was in love with me and expected me to love him in return. I would have treasured his friendship; I felt that it could have been a more beautiful friendship than any I had known – but now I left Tobelbad.*

Alma returned to Mahler at Toblach, where he was now thoroughly immersed in his Tenth Symphony. At the same time he was making anxious preparations for the first performance, in Munich, of the Eighth Symphony (which he had dedicated to Alma). It is ironic that he enjoyed probably the greatest triumph of his life at the very time that he came

closest to losing the woman who had inspired it all.

Mahler's composing hut at Toblach

Gropius, meanwhile, must have decided it was time to force the issue. He wrote a letter to Alma in which he frankly told her that he could not live without her, and that she must leave Mahler to be with him. He addressed the letter, whether accidentally or on purpose is not clear, to 'Herr Direktor Mahler'. Even this did not produce the confrontation Gropius hoped for, so he resorted to more desperate means.

In her autobiography, *My Life*, Alma tells how, during a walk, she saw Gropius hiding under a bridge. Apparently he had been in the neighborhood for some time, hoping to provoke a confrontation with Alma. Terrified, Alma went back and told Mahler, who – remarkably – replied, 'I'll go and get him'. Mahler set off to Toblach, found Gropius, and said simply, 'Come!' By now, night had fallen. Silently, the two men walked back, the composer leading the way with a lantern. Mahler found Alma and left her alone with Gropius, but after only a few minutes, Alma tells us, she became so anxious about Mahler that she went to his room. He was pacing back and forth, reading the Bible by candlelight. 'Whatever you decide,' he said, 'will be the right thing'. According to the version recorded in *My Life*, Alma felt she had no real choice. There was no question of life for her without Mahler, and certainly not with another man.

However, Alma's diaries and her letters to Gropius tell a somewhat different story: she had no intention of giving up the architect either. 'I know that I am living for the moment when I can be utterly and completely yours,' she wrote to him. She talked of having a child with Gropius so that she could 'lavish all my attention on that child until we can fall into each other's arms, joyously and for evermore, in security and without scruples'.

Mahler could no longer deny the significance Gropius had for his wife, and for the future of his marriage. He was so desperate to keep her that he tried just about every tactic he could: writing her effusive love poetry, taking out the manuscripts of the songs she had written before they were married and praising them, even persuading the publisher Emil Hertzka to print some of them; or there was simply outright denial, and feigned innocence. Emotionally Mahler was poised on a razor's edge. Alma remembers his constant need to reassure himself that she was still there (they slept in separate rooms):

Up in the night. He stood before me in the dark. I started as if I had seen a ghost. From now on, at mealtimes I had to fetch him from his shack. I did so with great caution, for he was afraid of losing me, afraid he had already lost me. And often, in his hyper-anxious state, he would lie on the ground in his shack, weeping. Like that, he explained, he felt closer to the earth.

In a note written from his composing hut, Mahler pleaded for her help. He also used a highly significant new term of endearment for her: 'mein Seitenspiel', hard to translate well but meaning something like 'my lyre-play'. This is significant because the same word is written on the sketch score of the

Mahler's handwritten score of the Tenth Symphony, with his words on the score caused by distress with Alma: 'Du allein weisst was es bedeutet. Ach! Ach! Got! Leb'wol mein Seitenspiel. Leb wol, Leb wol, Leb wol, Ach wol. Ach Ach'

179

Tenth Symphony, at the work's darkest point: the transition from the second scherzo to the finale.

My darling, my lyre-play,

I am possessed by dark spirits; they have cast me to the ground. Come and dispel them. Abide by me, my rod and staff. Come soon today, that I may rise up. Here I lie prostrate and await you; and silently I ask whether I may still hope for salvation, or whether I am to be damned.

Again, Alma is savior, redeemer: the very ideal he would be hymning in less than a month's time at the premiere of his Eighth Symphony. That note is just one of many indications that the emotional journey charted in the Tenth Symphony closely matched Mahler's mental turmoil at this time. The more one considers the sketches of the Tenth alongside what is known of Mahler's feelings at the time he was writing it, the clearer it becomes that, whatever Mahler's initial plans, the Tenth Symphony became the expression of his violent mood-swings, his ecstatic hopes and agonized fears for his relationship with Alma. One of the poems he poured out in that summer of 1910 reads like a motto for the new symphony: 'Let me condense the tremors of my yearning, / Th'eternity of bliss divine in your embrace, / Into one great song.'

The manuscripts are full of verbal confirmations: some clear, others wildly scribbled. Above and below the staves of the second scherzo are exclamations like 'The devil dances it with me', 'Farewell my lyre-play'; then in the finale are the poignant 'To live for you, to die for you', and, over the great sigh that ends the symphony, the single word 'Almschi', Mahler's habitual pet name for Alma. It is also evident from the sketches that these were not mere private outpourings.

At some point late in that summer Mahler changed his mind about the ending of the symphony. Originally it had finished in the key of B flat major, but then Mahler conceived the wonderful modulation that twists the last section back into F sharp major, the key of the symphony's first two movements. When he copied out the final pages of the sketch in the new key, he carefully re-inserted those words, 'To live for you, to die for you' and 'Almschi', in the exact equivalent places. Even in his emotional extremity, it seems, Mahler had an eye to posterity; or was it just that these annotations were now so crucial to his conception of the symphony that he could not imagine the music without them?

Whatever the reason, it was now clear to all around him that Mahler needed help. A friend arranged a meeting between Mahler and the great Viennese psychoanalyst Sigmund Freud (1856–1939) in Holland. At first compliant, Mahler then stalled, which Freud probably rightly interpreted as a symptom of panicked denial. Freud wrote firmly to Mahler: it was now or not at all. So the meeting took place. The two men had a long conversation. It did not take Freud much time to diagnose Mahler as having a mother fixation. They also discussed the conjunction of 'high tragedy and light amusement' in his music. Recalling the session fifteen years later, Freud continued:

> *Mahler suddenly said that now he understood why his music had always been prevented from achieving the highest rank through the noblest passages, those inspired by the most profound emotions being spoiled by intrusion of some commonplace melody.*

This remark is often quoted as though it really does explain that very characteristic feature of Mahler's music but, as

Michael Kennedy says, it is just 'too pat'. For one thing, is Mahler's music always 'spoiled' by these intrusions? Is not that very juxtaposition of profundity and apparent banality one of the things that makes Mahler so fascinating? If the root cause is to be found in Mahler's own personal pathology, a response to a unique traumatic event, why then does such juxtaposition make emotional sense to so many listeners today? In any case, writers very different from Mahler have noted that 'banal' music can, in the right circumstances, be strangely affecting. Noël Coward had the famous line, 'How potent cheap music is'. Three centuries earlier, Sir Thomas Browne (author of *The Anatomy of Melancholy*) made this very Mahlerian observation: 'Even that vulgar and tavern music, which makes one man merry, another mad, strikes in me a deep fit of devotion'. Once again, in charting his own emotional experience, Mahler had uncovered something that can speak to all of us.

'One Great Song': The Tenth Symphony

Even though Mahler never finished the full orchestral score of his Tenth Symphony, his poetic prayer for the power to 'condense' all his hopes and terrors 'into one great song' was, in effect, answered. Properly understood, the sketches show that the work's leading melodic line, its 'great song', stands complete; for most of its length, the harmonies, counterpoints and main orchestral colors are indicated quite clearly. Moreover, Mahler's orchestral style is so idiosyncratic that, in places, it is only necessary to look at a phrase or chord to know immediately the kind of sound he had in mind: a shrill piccolo clarinet here, muted trumpets there, rich string polyphony or the liquid tones of the harp. It is clear enough that the Tenth was on the way to being one of Mahler's greatest symphonies, perhaps the greatest of them all. It has all the intensity of Symphony No. 9, and a better formal balance: the arch-like structure (*Adagio*–scherzo–*Allegretto moderato*–scherzo–*Adagio*) is as satisfying an overall structure as that of the 'classical' Sixth, while its emotional narrative is if anything even more gripping.

From the very start the intensity and the imaginative audacity of the Tenth Symphony are astonishing. It begins with a ghostly, groping, tonally rootless theme for unaccompanied violas that would not be out of place in a late work by Shostakovich. The main body of this great **Adagio** alternates tortured aspiration (some of Mahler's most harmonically advanced music) with sardonic, deflated dance tunes. Eventually, when it seems that the potential of this alternation has been exhausted, there is a huge, terrifying, full-orchestral passage, reaching its climax on an immense piled-up dissonance, with a painfully sustained high trumpet note and screaming high violins: a cry of despair or terror, torn from the heart. This yields to a gentler, soothing coda, with a warmer, tonally centered version of the great nine-note dissonance built up quietly on strings and harp, then resolving quietly in the home major key.

CD 2
track 7

www.naxosbooks.com

If it is Mahler's harmonic 'modernism' that impresses in the first movement, it is his sheer rhythmic inventiveness that stands out in the first scherzo. In this movement, written the year before Stravinsky began his rhythmically innovatory *The Rite of Spring*, the meter keeps shifting: three long beats in one bar, two in the next, five shorter beats in the one after that, and so on. Mahler had never written music of such rhythmic complexity before, and combined with his full contrapuntal skill it creates tremendous energy. The scherzo ends with a magnificent upsurge, culminating in an ecstatic three-note horn call, derived from the main theme of the first movement. It seems that this will be the triumph of life but Mahler, being Mahler, contradicts it immediately. The little *Allegretto moderato* third movement has the enigmatic title 'Purgatorio', against which, in the initial sketches, Mahler added the words 'or Inferno'. This weird dance movement takes its basic running accompaniment from an earlier setting from *Des Knaben Wunderhorn*, a spooky little song entitled 'Das irdische Leben' ('Earthly Life'), about a child who dies from starvation. Was the mother-fixated Mahler identifying himself with the child's plight as he desperately tried to hold on to his 'Mater Gloriosa', Alma? There are unmistakable cries of pain from the full orchestra in the middle section, before the more or less exact return of the first section. Even here, Mahler's sense of the grand formal container does not fail him: centrally placed at the hub of the work, the *Purgatorio*'s A–B–A structure mirrors the Tenth Symphony's overall arch form.

The second scherzo (it has no title in the sketches but its formal character is clear) is even more diabolical than the rondo 'Burleske' of Symphony No. 9. Here there are strong echoes of the opening movement of *Das Lied von der Erde*, especially of the phrase associated with the words 'joy and singing wither and die'. The end of the movement, which links directly into the finale, is one of Mahler's most extraordinary passages. On the sketch Mahler wrote the words, 'You alone know what it means'. Alma certainly did know what it meant. The inspiration was the memory of an event they both witnessed from their rooms at New York's Hotel Majestic. At the time, Alma was in another room, talking to a young art student:

Hearing a confused noise, we leaned out of the window and saw a long procession in the broad street along the side of Central Park. It was the funeral cortège of a fireman, of whose heroic death we had read in the newspaper. The chief mourners were almost immediately below us when the procession halted, and the master of ceremonies stepped forward and gave a short address. From our eleventh-floor window we could only guess what he said. There was a brief pause and then a stroke on the muffled drum, followed by dead silence. The procession then moved forward and all was over.

The scene brought tears to our eyes and I looked anxiously at Mahler's window. But he too was leaning out and his face was streaming with tears. The brief drum stroke impressed him so deeply that he used it in the Tenth Symphony.

It is all there in the Tenth Symphony: the muffled drum strokes, the long 'dead' silences. In the closing pages of the Ninth Symphony, Mahler imaginatively lived through the experience of dying. Here he dares to go even further. This is perhaps the closest music has ever come to a vision of the utter extinction of death: total nothingness. Surely the 'one great song' cannot survive an encounter like this? Yet it does. Grotesquely at first, a slow melodic line rises in the deep bass, with hollow harmonies underlined by two contrabassoons. The melody rises still further through the orchestra. It is as though the song has resurrected in the very face of black emptiness. Even in Mahler's psychological hell, singing is still possible. Eventually it reaches its almost unbelievably touching apotheosis in a long, quiet flute solo (the composer Berthold Goldschmidt once remarked that this passage alone justified the reconstruction and performance of Mahler's Tenth Symphony). The struggle is not over yet, and eventually there is a return of the shattering dissonance from the climax of the first movement. This resolves gradually into the final, wonderfully tender love song, with its concluding great orchestral sigh for 'Almschi'. Was Mahler perhaps thinking here of one of the most famous of all the verses in the Old Testament (words he might possibly have heard read in the synagogue in childhood): 'For love is strong as death'?

The finale of the Tenth Symphony may be the ultimate answer to those who accuse Mahler of being negative, egoistic, merely self-indulgent. Of course he is self-dramatizing here, as always; and yet in the process of expressing his own fears, agonies, joys, longings (feelings that so often find echoes in his listeners of today) he is able to sing such exquisite songs of consolation – of love, life and hope. The 'one great song' survives even the bleak vision of extinction that opens the finale. Of course, had Mahler lived he would have worked further on the symphony, probably fleshing it out in the orchestral score during spare moments in New York or during the following year's summer holiday; but we should be thankful that he got as far as he did, and that what we have is so magnificent and moving.

The End

As it turned out, the discovery of Alma's love for Gropius was indeed the blow that felled Mahler 'as a tree is felled', not in an instant, but in a gradually accelerating, unstoppable fall. On returning to New York from Toblach at the end of October 1910, Mahler's health problems grew worse and worse. The septic throat and feverish symptoms returned in force at Christmas, and again in February the following year. A Viennese doctor, Joseph Fränkel, was called. Fränkel immediately recognized the seriousness of the condition and ordered tests. The diagnosis was streptococcal infection: not necessarily fatal today, but almost certainly so for Mahler. Fränkel advised him to go to Paris to consult an eminent bacteriologist. On arrival in Paris, Mahler rallied spectacularly, and even started making plans for a holiday in Egypt. This is how Alma remembered it:

*I stared at him in utter astonishment. It seemed literally to be
a miracle. He had not done anything for himself for months.
My mother and I had had almost to carry him from the boat.
And now I sent for Mama and Moll, whose love for Mahler
was nothing short of idolatry. We all laughed and wept for joy.
It seemed he was saved.*

*He talked with great excitement about future productions
during breakfast:* The Barber of Baghdad *[by Peter Cornelius].
It would be marvelous; and he began to develop his ideas for
making it go. He jumped up (a pang of dread clutched at my
throat) and abruptly ordered an electric automobile. He got
into it as a man recovered, and got out, after an hour's drive,
as a man at death's door.*

A Viennese blood specialist was sent for: Dr Franz Chvostek.
He immediately ordered Mahler to a sanatorium in Vienna.
Sometimes Mahler grew excited and talked at great speed,
but it was clear that he was growing weaker. One of his last
acts was to entrust the sketches of the Tenth Symphony to
Alma. It seems that he wanted the music to survive him. He
also expressed the wish to be buried beside Putzi in Vienna's
Grinzing Cemetery. This wish was carried out. Mahler died
on 18 May 1911, less than two months short of his fifty-
first birthday. Like Beethoven, he died in the middle of a
thunderstorm. According to Alma, his last word was 'Mozart',
said twice with a faint smile on his lips. Today, his tomb at
Grinzing is a place of pilgrimage. The inscription simply
reads 'Gustav Mahler'. That is all. For what more is necessary?
When the architect Christopher Wren was buried in his own
St. Paul's Cathedral, his inscription read: 'Si monumentum
requiris, circumspice' ('If you require a monument, look
around you'). With a slight adaptation, this would do equally
well for Mahler: if you need a monument to this great
composer, just listen.

Personalities

Bahr-Mildenburg, Anna (1872–1947): Austrian dramatic soprano noted for her performances of Wagnerian roles. She sang under Mahler in Hamburg and Vienna, and she had an intense affair with him.

Bauer-Lechner, Natalie (1858–1921): Austrian viola player and member of the Soldat-Roeger Quartet. A close friend and confidante of Mahler until his marriage to Alma in 1902. Her *Erinnerungen an Gustav Mahler* (1923) is very informative, but unfortunately is not currently available in English translation.

Berg, Alban (1885–1935): Austrian composer, pupil of Schoenberg and passionate devotee of Mahler. He described Mahler's Sixth Symphony as 'the only Sixth', despite Beethoven's 'Pastoral', and imitated its 'fatal' hammer blows in his Three Pieces for Orchestra (1913–14).

Brahms, Johannes (1833–1897): German 'Classical-Romantic' composer and outspoken opponent of Wagnerism. He admired Mahler's conducting and befriended him in his last years.

Bruckner, Anton (1824–1896): Austrian composer famed for his symphonies and religious works. He was a friend and musical mentor to Mahler during the latter's years at the Vienna Conservatory.

Bulöw, Hans von (1830–1894): German conductor, pianist and noted caustic wit. He championed Mahler as a conductor after hearing him at the Hamburg Opera.

Chvostek, Franz (1864–1944): Viennese physician and expert on blood diseases. He treated Mahler on the composer's return to Vienna in 1911.

Conried, Heinrich (1848–1909): Manager of The Metropolitan Opera, New York (1903–8), responsible for recruiting Mahler as the company's musical director.

Cooke, Deryck (1919–1976): British critic, scholar and influential BBC producer. His 'performing version' of Mahler's incomplete Tenth Symphony is the one most widely heard today.

Epstein, Julius (1832–1926): Austrian pianist, and professor at the Vienna Conservatory (1867–1901). One of the first to recognize Mahler's exceptional talent, he encouraged him and helped him to find financial support during his student years.

Fränkel, Joseph (1867–1920): Viennese physician, who moved to New York in 1893. He examined Mahler in February 1911 and realized the fatal nature of his illness.

Freud, Sigmund (1856–1939): Austrian psychiatrist and father of modern psychoanalysis. Mahler consulted him in 1910, when Freud diagnosed the composer as suffering from a mother complex.

Gabrilovitch, Ossip (1878–1936): Russian-born pianist and conductor, an enthusiast of Mahler's music and also of Alma.

Gatti-Casazza, Giulio (1869–1940): Italian impresario, and director of The Metropolitan Opera, New York (1908–35). He was a champion of Mahler's rival, Toscanini, and his appointment at The Metropolitan hastened Mahler's departure.

Gropius, Walter (1883–1969): Influential German architect. His affair with Alma brought about Mahler's final marital crisis. Gropius married Alma in 1915.

Jahn, Wilhelm (1834–1900): Conductor and musical director at the Vienna Court Opera from 1881 until 1897, when he was succeeded by Mahler.

Krzyzanowski, Rudolf (1862–1911): Austrian conductor. A close friend of Mahler during his Conservatory years, he was Mahler's assistant at Hamburg (1896–7) and court conductor at Weimar (1898–1907).

Lipiner, Siegfried (1856–1911): Philosopher, dramatist and poet, he was the young Mahler's intellectual mentor.

Mahler, Alma (*née* Schindler) (1879–1964): Writer, composer and daughter of the painter Emil Schindler. She met Mahler in 1901 and married him the following year. She was the inspiration for much of Mahler's later music.

Mahler, Anna ('Gucki') (1904–1988): Mahler's second daughter.

Mahler, Bernhard (1827–1888): The composer's father, who

became manager of a successful distillery. Mahler described Bernhard as 'brutal', yet the composer's directorial style was probably much influenced by his father.

Mahler, Ernst (1861–1874): The composer's brother. Ernst's early death made a powerful impression on Mahler and on his music.

Mahler, Justine ('Justi') (1868–1938): Mahler's favorite sister. She kept house for him in his early years in Vienna. She married the violinist Arnold Rosé in 1902.

Mahler, Leopoldine ('Poldi') (1863–1889): Sister of the composer. Mentally unstable and prone to hallucinations of death, she died of a brain tumor.

Mahler, Maria ('Putzi') (1902–1907): Mahler's first and favorite daughter. Her death at the age of four shattered him.

Mahler, Marie (*née* Hermann) (1837–1888): The composer's long-suffering mother. Mahler adored her, it is said, to the point of fixation.

Manheit, Jacques (dates unknown): Baritone in the Olmütz Municipal Theatre. He later joined Mahler in Budapest.

Mengelberg, Willem (1871–1951): Dutch conductor of the Amsterdam Concertgebouw Orchestra. He was an important early champion of Mahler's music.

Moll, Carl (1861–1945): Austrian painter, and pupil of Alma's father Emil Schindler. After Schindler's death he married Alma's mother and became her stepfather.

Nietzsche, Friedrich (1844–1900): German philosopher and creator of the concept of the *Übermensch* ('Superman'). Mahler's Third Symphony was partly inspired by Nietzsche's writings and contains a setting of words from his *Also sprach Zarathustra* ('Thus Spake Zarathustra'), though Mahler's admiration for him was not unqualified.

Nikisch, Arthur (1855–1922): Famous Hungarian conductor. Mahler became his assistant at Leipzig in 1886.

Papier, Rosa (1858–1932): Austrian mezzo-soprano at the Vienna Opera until her retirement in 1891, after which she became an influential teacher.

Pollini, Bernhard (1838–1897): German tenor and theatre manager. He was director at the Hamburg Opera from 1873.

Roller, Alfred (1864–1935): Stage designer recruited by Mahler at the Vienna Court Opera in 1903. He created renowned productions of operas by Mozart, Beethoven and Wagner.

Rott, Hans (1858–1884): Exceptionally gifted Austrian composer and friend of Mahler at the Vienna Conservatory. He died insane.

Rückert, Friedrich (1788–1866): German Romantic poet. Mahler was one of several composers who found his verse especially conducive to musical setting.

Schindler, Emil Jakob (1842–1892): Important Austrian painter and much beloved father of Alma.

Schoenberg, Arnold (1874–1951): Austrian composer and

pioneer of the 'twelve-note' method of composing. Initially antagonistic to Mahler's music, he became a passionate admirer.

Schopenhauer, Arthur (1788–1860): German philosopher, and probably the most important intellectual influence on Wagner's later music dramas. The young Mahler was much impressed by his ideas.

Sibelius, Jean (1865–1957): Finnish composer and conductor, noted for his symphonies and symphonic poems. His account of his discussion with Mahler about the nature of the symphony is brief but very revealing.

Strauss, Richard (1864–1949): German composer, especially celebrated for his operas, songs and orchestral tone poems. His friendship with Mahler and championship of his music was important, but Mahler's attitude to him was equivocal.

Toscanini, Arturo (1867–1957): Outstanding Italian conductor. In 1908 he replaced Mahler at The Metropolitan Opera, New York.

Wagner, Richard (1813–1883): Hugely influential German composer and conductor. His concept of the Gesamtkunstwerk ('total work of art') revolutionized opera composition. Despite Wagner's notorious anti-Semitism, Mahler was dedicated to his music, especially *Tristan und Isolde*.

Walter, Bruno (1876–1962): Eminent Austrian conductor. He was assistant to Mahler in Hamburg and Vienna, and became a close friend and lifelong advocate of his music.

Wolf, Hugo (1860–1903): Austrian composer, especially noted for his songs. He was a friend of Mahler at the Vienna Conservatory. Always unstable, he died insane.

Zemlinsky, Alexander von (1871–1942): Austrian composer and conductor. He became a close friend of Mahler, despite losing Alma to him in 1901.

Zuckerkandl, Bertha (*née* Szeps) (1863–1945): Austrian writer and wife of the Viennese anatomist Emil Zuckerkandl. It was at one of her dinner parties that the alleged first meeting between Mahler and Alma took place.

Selected Bibliography

Blaukopf, Herta, ed., trans. Edmund Jephcott, *Gustav Mahler – Richard Strauss, Correspondence 1888–1911*, London, 1984

Carr, Jonathan, *The Real Mahler*, London, 1997

Cooke, Deryck, *Gustav Mahler, An Introduction to His Music*, London, 1980

Del Mar, Norman, *Mahler's Sixth Symphony – A Study*, London, 1980

Kennedy, Michael, *Mahler* ('The Master Musicians Series'), London, 1974

Lebrecht, Norman, ed., *Mahler Remembered*, London, 1987

Mahler, Alma, ed. Donald Mitchell and Knud Martner, trans. Basil Creighton, *Gustav Mahler, Memories and Letters*, London, 1990

Mahler, Gustav, ed. Henry-Louis de la Grange and Günther Weiss, rev. & trans. Anthony Beaumont, *Gustav Mahler, Letters to His Wife*, London, 2004

Mitchell, Donald, *Gustav Mahler, Vol. I, The Early Years*, London, 1958

Mitchell, Donald, *Gustav Mahler, Vol. II, The Wunderhorn Years*, London, 1975

Mitchell, Donald, *Gustav Mahler, Vol. III, Songs and Symphonies of Life and Death*, London, 2002

Reilly, Edward R., *Gustav Mahler and Guido Adler, Records of a Friendship*, Cambridge, 1982

Glossary

Adagietto   Diminutive of *adagio*. Hence 'slow, but not as slow as *adagio*'. By calling the fourth movement of his Fifth Symphony *Adagietto*, Mahler may have meant to signify 'a little slow movement'.

Adagio   Italian for 'slow', 'at ease'. The slow movement of a symphony is often referred to as an *adagio*.

Allegro   Italian for 'quick', 'lively'. In a symphony, an *allegro* is a fast movement, usually of a serious or energetic nature.

Celesta (or Celeste)   A small keyboard instrument, in which steel bars are struck by hammers, giving a delicate, bell-like sound. Mahler was the first composer to employ the celesta in a symphony (No. 6).

Lieder   German for 'songs' (singular 'Lied'). The word is used to identify the tradition of art songs in German, beginning with Beethoven's cycle *An die ferne Geliebte* ('To the Distant Beloved') and continuing as far as Richard Strauss and Berg in the twentieth century.

Music drama   Wagner's term for a new vision of opera, in which all music, drama, poetry, song and painting are fused to form a 'total work of art' (*Gesamtkunstwerk*).

Counterpoint (adj. Contrapuntal)   A musical style in which two or more parts, or 'voices', move independently, each with its own validity as a melodic or thematic line in its own right, creating a highly dynamic but still coherent overall texture. It is therefore more complex than the simpler tune-plus-accompaniment texture.

Pizzicato   Italian for 'pinched' or 'plucked'. A style of string playing in which the strings are plucked with the fingers rather than being stroked with the bow.

Rondo   From the Italian for 'round'. A movement, possibly with several contrasted themes, in which one main theme returns intermittently, thus giving the argument a circular or 'round' character.

Scherzo   Italian for 'joke', 'jest'. A symphonic movement, usually in three-time, of a particularly lively, dance-like character. It developed from the Classical minuet. Beethoven's earliest scherzos often have a vigorous, sometimes savagely humorous nature, but by the titanic scherzo of his Ninth Symphony, comedy had been largely left behind. Scherzos often have a contrasting middle section or sections known as a trio.

Song cycle   A sequence of songs, which can sometimes be performed separately, but which are best understood as part of a larger entity. Sometimes, as in Schubert's *Die schöne Müllerin*, Schumann's *Dichterliebe* or Mahler's *Lieder eines fahrenden Gesellen*, the cycle as a whole appears to relate a story. Other song cycles are unified more by a poetic idea or collection of ideas, for example Mahler's *Kindertotenlieder*.

Symphonic poem/ Tone poem   A substantial orchestral work in which the character and form of the musical argument are decided not by Classical models but by literary programmes or ideas. The form was pioneered by Liszt and developed by Tchaikovsky, Richard Strauss and Sibelius.

Symphony   From the latter half of the eighteenth century, an extended work for orchestra, usually in several contrasting movements. During the Romantic era it came to be seen as a vehicle for the loftiest instrumental thoughts. Following the example of Beethoven's Ninth Symphony, some composers, notably Mahler, also included sung texts for chorus and/or vocal soloists.

Annotations of CD Tracks

CD 1

☐ Symphony No. 5. **Movement 3: Scherzo**

Mahler famously said that 'the symphony must be like the world. It must embrace everything.' But it is rare to find an individual movement that embraces as much as the scherzo of the Fifth Symphony. Mahler himself wondered how audiences would react to 'this chaos, which is constantly giving birth to new worlds and promptly destroying them again? What should they make of these primeval noises, this rushing, roaring, raging sea, these dancing stars, these ebbing, shimmering, gleaming waves?' The mood veers from wild, even crazy elation to deep melancholic gloom – yet everything is achieved with the scintillating virtuosity of a master magician.

☐ Lieder eines fahrenden Gesellen. **No. 4: 'Die zwei blauen Augen'**

A doomed love affair stands behind Mahler's first orchestral song cycle, *Lieder eines fahrenden Gesellen* ('Songs of a Wayfarer'). Like the girl in the title of the fourth and final song, Mahler's beloved, Johanna Richter, had two striking blue eyes. The cycle's protagonist is a typical 'romantic outcast'. Spurned by the beloved, he walks away from her wedding celebrations and tries to find a new kind of happiness through a oneness with nature. But he fails, and the final song, with its unmistakable funeral tread, shows him bidding farewell to love, to hope, and perhaps also to life itself.

☐ Symphony No. 1. **Movement 3: Feierlich und gemessen, ohne zu schleppen**

Mahler's early symphonies and songs are often closely interwoven. The First Symphony, originally entitled 'Titan', contains two explicit and substantial quotations from *Lieder eines fahrenden Gesellen*. The crucial reference occurs at the heart of the strange, sardonic third movement, which combines the funeral tread from 'Die zwei blauen Augen' with sombre, imitative variations on the old song *Frère Jacques*. A sudden sarcastic burst of Jewish Klezmer music (often heard at wedding celebrations) leads eventually to a lightly reworked version of the despairing ending of 'Die zwei blauen Augen'. By invoking Jewish wedding music, Mahler here identifies the hero of the song cycle still more closely with himself.

4, 5 Symphony No. 3
Movement 4: Sehr langsam. Misterioso. 'O Mensch, gib Acht!'
Movement 5: Lustig im Tempo und keck im Ausdruck. 'Es sungen drei Engel'

The linked fourth and fifth movements of the Third Symphony show how Mahler brings extreme contrasts, sometimes even contradictions, into the 'embrace' of his music. In the fourth movement the contralto sings the climactic verses from Nietzsche's *Also sprach Zarathustra* ('Thus Spake Zarathustra'), which tells how the ideal philosopher can exult in the face of both the world's joy and its pain. But this runs straight into a depiction of simple faith, compassion and forgiveness that the 'anti-Christian' Nietzsche would have disdained.

6 Symphony No. 7. **Movement 2: Nachtmusik I**

Like the Nietzsche movement from the Third Symphony, the second movement of Mahler's Symphony No. 7 is a 'song of the night', this time partly inspired by Rembrandt's painting *The Night Watch*. But while the earlier movement is all rapt contemplation, the mood of this 'night music' is more complex, full of half-lights and weird phantasmagoria, like the teeming woodwind chorus that grows out of the opening mysterious horn calls. This music is also full of riddles. Why are there echoes of the Sixth Symphony's major–minor 'fate' motif, and of its cowbells (here stripped of their former ethereal 'Alpine' magic)? This music is endlessly fascinating, yet at heart it remains inscrutable.

7 Symphony No. 4. Movement 4: **Sehr behaglich. 'Das himmlische Leben'**

On one level, the last movement of the Fourth Symphony is exactly what Mahler said it was: a strangely touching portrayal of a 'child's view of heaven', to be performed 'absolutely without parody'. At the same time it makes a superbly logical culmination to a great symphony, about as far removed as possible from the romantic notion of a symphonic finale being a 'heroic apotheosis'. As elsewhere in the Fourth Symphony, the depiction of innocent childhood happiness is crossed with shadows. But everything is done with remarkable subtlety and delicacy.

CD 2

☐ Rückert Lieder. **No. 3: 'Ich bin der Welt abhanden gekommen'**

One of Mahler's greatest orchestral songs, 'Ich bin der Welt abhanden gekommen', gives a taste of the mental freedom that he found during his summer 'composing holidays' in the magnificent isolation of the Austrian Alps. It was a time when he could forget the irritations and frustrations of his work as an opera conductor and become truly, as the song says, 'lost to the world'. The descending violin line that accompanies the singer's final phrases ('in my love, in my song') returns in full at the end of the *Adagietto* from the Fifth Symphony, another indication of a 'message' hidden in the wordless textures of Mahler's orchestral music.

☐ Symphony No. 5. **Movement 4: Adagietto**

The most popular of all Mahler's orchestral 'songs without words', this lovely movement for strings and harp is surely a love song for his new wife, Alma. Almost certainly he meant her to recognize the quotation from 'Ich bin der Welt...' (see above) in the final bars and read its message. But the *Adagietto* is no simple expression of the happiness of new-found love. There is tremendous yearning, sometimes deep sadness, in this music too. It seems the ever-complicated, death-haunted Mahler could not experience love without contemplating the possibility of its loss, hardly surprising in a symphony that begins with one of Mahler's grimmest funeral marches.

☐, ☐ Kindertotenlieder
No. 4: 'Oft denk' ich...'
No. 5: 'In diesem Wetter'

That the ideas of love and loss were intimately connected in Mahler's mind is further borne out by the orchestral song cycle, *Kindertotenlieder* ('Songs on the Deaths of Children'). Though the cycle was begun before Mahler's beloved daughter Maria ('Putzi') was conceived, Alma was horrified by what she saw as Mahler's 'tempting fate' in these songs, and her misgivings seemed to be confirmed when Maria died at the age of four. Unlike Alma, though, Mahler had grown up in a house where childhood mortality was a simple fact of life. That may help to explain the aching poignancy of these extraordinarily beautiful songs.

5 Symphony No. 6. **Movement 2: Scherzo. Wuchtig**

Rarely do innocence and evil confront each other so dramatically as in the scherzo of the Sixth Symphony, originally entitled 'Tragic'. Pounding drumbeats and mocking, sneering woodwind with clattering 'devilish laughter' on xylophone drive the movement forward relentlessly. Later a curiously naïve woodwind tune (its beat limping between three and four beats in a bar) suggests comic, childish games, but these are savagely dismissed by the opening music, which seems increasingly menacing with each appearance. After a shrill climactic chord, the childlike tune fragments grotesquely, ending with the skeletal grunting of the contrabassoon and three hollow notes on timpani.

6 Das Lied von der Erde. **Movement 2: 'Der Einsame im Herbst'**

The death of 'Putzi' and the diagnosis of Mahler's heart problem in 1907 clearly left their mark on the great 'song-symphony' *Das Lied von der Erde* ('The Song of the Earth'). Mahler had to change his summer composing routine (no cycling or long walks), and the loss of his favorite daughter heightened painfully his sense of being 'lost to the world'. That text of this second movement, with its central image of 'The lonely one in autumn', resonated powerfully with Mahler, as did the lines 'My heart is tired. / My little lamp splutters out'.

7 Symphony No. 10. **Movement 1: Adagio**

In the last full year of his life, Mahler struggled to express his love for Alma in 'one great song of love', ironically unaware (at first) that his marriage was under threat. Death prevented him from putting the finishing touches to his Tenth Symphony, but what he left is near enough to completion to give an idea of what an astonishing work it would have been – perhaps the most emotionally extreme of all his symphonies. Like the work as a whole, the opening *Adagio* journeys through desperate longing, icy visions of death, and convulsive terror to final hope of renewal and peace.

Index